T0150291

FILIGREE

PERMISSIONS:

Tishani Doshi: "Everyone Loves a Dead Girl", "Coastal Life" and "My Grandmother Never Ate a Potato in Her Life", from *Girls Are Coming Out of the Woods* (Bloodaxe Books, 2018)
Roy McFarlane: "Dancing with Ghosts", from *The Healing Next Time* (Nine Arches Press, 2018)

ACKNOWLEDGEMENTS

Thank you to those who helped with making the book happen:
Tanyaradzwa April Guvi
Megan McCaskill (intern from Leicester University)
Dorothea Smartt, Panya Banjoko and Olive Senior who worked with poets to bring *Filigree* poems to fruition

FILIGREE

CONTEMPORARY BLACK BRITISH POETRY

Edited by Nii Ayikwei Parkes

Inscribe series editor: Kadija Sessay

P E E P A L   T R E E

First published in Great Britain in 2018
by Inscribe an imprint of
Peepal Tree Press Ltd
17 King's Avenue
Leeds LS6 1QS
UK

ISBN 9781845234263

Supported using public funding by
ARTS COUNCIL
ENGLAND

CONTENTS

DOROTHY WANG

PREFACE
FILIGREE: CONTEMPORARY BLACK BRITISH POETRY

It has become a truism that the single most salient social factor
in the UK is class. Race is an American problem. Yet European
colonialism and capitalism – the two most determinant histori-
cal forces that have produced the world we live in today – were,
are, and always have been intrinsically bound up in the nexus of
class and race, both internally and in connection with one another
(think racialised labour and the genocide of indigenous peoples for
land dispossession).

It was the British who attained the honour of perfecting modern
– that is, racialised – colonialism into its most powerful, far-reach-
ing and durable forms, the double-headed hydra of settler colo-
nialism and extractive colonialism.[1] At its apex, Britain's was the
largest empire in history. Every person on this planet lives in the
wake of the structures, logics, ideologies, and aesthetic principles
bestowed by this domination.

---

1. Coincident with the rise of these 'external-facing' forms of colonialism
were Elizabeth I's draft proclamations in 1596 and 1601 calling for the re-
moval of 'Negroes and blackamoors' from 'the realm of England':https://
www.bl.uk/collection-items/draft-proclamation-on-the-expulsion-of-ne-
groes-and-blackamoors-1601 and http://www.nationalarchives.gov.uk/path-
ways/blackhistory/early_times/transcripts/deportation_van_senden.htm.
See also Miranda Kaufmann, 'Caspar van Senden, Sir Thomas Sherley and
the "Blackamoor" Project', *Historical Research*, 81.212 (May 2008): 366-371;
Emily C. Bartels, 'Too Many Blackamoors: Deportation, Discrimination,
and Elizabeth I'. *Studies in English Literature, 1500-1900*, 46.2 (2006): 305-
322. Thanks to John Keene for this point.

A 2014 YouGov poll found that 59% of the British public feels that the empire was something to be proud of, three times as many as those who felt it was something of which to be ashamed (19%).[2] What David Olusoga calls 'our collective amnesia'[3] has worked in tandem with conscious efforts by those in power to whitewash history and produce a sepia-tinted fantasy redolent of sandalwood.[4]

It may be comforting for Britons, including (or especially) well-meaning white liberal elites – what the poet Tishani Doshi calls '[b]enevolent people'[5] – to see their society as a small social democratic and progressive country, not unlike Sweden. The days of the Raj and of the Union Jack flying over Kingston, Ceylon, and Zanzibar are erased or a hazy romantic thing of the past.

Yet, anyone who bothers to scratch the surface can see that there is a clear and continuous link across time and space between Jamestown, plantations in the American South and in the Caribbean, the Opium Wars, Sand Creek, Jallianwala Bagh, Mau Mau detention camps, Oswald Mosely (the Queen's distant cousin), Windrush, the Troubles, David Oluwale, Stephen Lawrence, and, now, Brexit. Indeed it was only in 2015 that the final payment of the £20 million (equivalent to £300 billion today) compensation package given to white slaveowners and their descendants (in-

---

2   https://yougov.co.uk/news/2014/07/26/britain-proud-its-empire/

3   David Olusoga, 'Wake up, Britain. Should the empire really be a source of pride?', *The Guardian*, Jan. 23, 2016, https://www.theguardian.com/commentisfree/2016/jan/23/britain-empire-pride-poll.

4   See, for example, historian Carolyn Elkins' piece 'My critics ignored evidence of torture in Mau Mau detention camps', *The Guardian*, April 14, 2011, https://www.theguardian.com/commentisfree/2011/apr/14/torture-mau-mau-camps-kenya, and also her book *Imperial Reckoning: The Untold Story of Britain's Gulag in Kenya* (New York: Henry Holt, 2005). It is only one of many examples, too numerous to cite, of the refusal on the part of some British to acknowledge colonial atrocities, especially those in the recent past. Vacationers in the Caribbean have no qualms about staying at resorts called 'plantations'.

5   From her poem 'Everyone Loves a Dead Girl' in this volume.

cluding David Cameron) was finally paid off by British taxpayers.[6] Barclays Bank, which helped to underwrite the slave trade, is still raking in profits. Scotland is yet to be independent. South Africa has a long road to recovery (whatever that might mean). And Gaza is an open-air prison.

'Yes, but what does this unfortunate history have to do with poetry?' one might ask.

First, at the very concrete level of existence, colonised peoples – whether chattel slaves, indentured servants, coolies, those paid subsistence wages in colonies, prisoners, other forms of subjugated labour, or simply nonpersons – were meant to have lives that did not include poetry. Under conditions of bare existence in which their only function was to work to increase the profits of their colonisers,[7] most struggled simply to survive: 'an empire somewhere wants to ride my shoulders. wants to / mount my back. wound man's spirit, break man in' ('Maroon', Michael Campbell). And even when they did get an education, it was one that told them in so many ways that they did not have the mind or imaginative capacity for poetry.

The overweening ideological, political and social thought and practices of a society cannot but affect the ideas governing all matter of forms in that society, including aesthetic ones. Racialised thinking and material practices, like capitalist ones, undergird and inform not only national borders, laws, military and administrative organisations and a variety of institutional structures, but categories of thought, psychic landscapes, and our ideas about artistic value – including, yes, poetry. It goes without saying that a black or brown or yellow person thought to be intellectually and morally

---

6   Kris Manjapra, 'When will Britain face up to its crimes against humanity?', *The Guardian*, Mar. 29, 2018. https://www.theguardian.com/news/2018/mar/29/slavery-abolition-compensation-when-will-britain-face-up-to-its-crimes-against-humanity.

7   Of course, under capitalism, all workers, including white ones, are expected to create profit for enterprises but race added yet another – some would argue the main – justification for oppression and one that was 'scientifically' rationalised.

inferior cannot be presumed to be able to write great poetry – or poetry at all.

English itself is, of course, a language powerfully shaped by centuries of colonialism (the centrality of the discipline of English is more directly a result of imperial might). The current globality of English as a language of commerce is also a function of the former military and economic force of that once-formidable empire and, now, of its most successful settler colonial spin-off across the Atlantic. English-language poetry derives as much of its lustre from the power of the Empire as it does from the prowess of Shakespeare. And The Bard was not just Exhibit A of the greatness of the British Empire but an active cudgel, alongside actual military weaponry, in subjugating colonised peoples: his poetic genius was used as a justification for the inherent superiority of the English (white Anglo-Saxon) mind and imagination.

Indeed, the unspoken assumption behind what was and is considered great English poetry is that it is white, English, and male and that the 'universal' poetic speaker is also white and male (and usually not working-class). The norms of English poetry with all its traditions and inherent assumptions (including racial) determines the linguistic and formal options that are available for nonwhite poets to write themselves into being – often according to a script. Even a personal poem to a baby daughter can present a dilemma about form (and audience):

> Your mother wants the poems about you;
> fatherhood-bildungsroman-eulogies,
> clever villanelles where, like you, the refrain
> reinvents the stanzas of our narrative,
> a reassuring haven for us to return to.
> She wants sonnets that mirror the paradox
> […]
> But I haven't any poems, save fragments [. . .]
> ('From a Father to a Daughter', Samatar Elmi)

Colonial and racialised ideas intrinsic to the norms and assumptions of English poetics write into being the (poetic) interiority of those deemed racially inferior. But as the rather wistful tone of this excerpt shows, the colonisation of the psyche does not result in a simple and monochromatically razed interior but one that is marked by yearning and melancholy.

Thus, while Black British poets recognise that they have been written into a white poetic history that was not theirs and was never meant for them, they are also left with the colonial legacy of English poetry, written by English, Irish, Scottish, Americans, West Indians, Asians, Africans, among others, which mediates even the most personal moments of their lives:

> [...] We are marooned here.
> Seamus Heaney is still in the shed. Plath
> and Hughes drop in, revitalise
> our meetings as they always do, shine
> a light on our constant tussles with ideas and form.
> Sometimes Walcott returns, like the *Wide Sargasso Sea* [...]
> ('Voyage in the Dark', Maggie Harris)

Here, the speaker tries to (re)connect through poetry with a woman – mother, friend, lover? – who is no longer fully herself. These lines illustrate how English language, its literary forms, and the assumptions behind those forms inform our intimate relationships to others and to ourselves.

A major effect of British, and more generally European, colonialism, long after the military firepower has receded, has been to turn historical reality into its distorted mirror opposite – and that version made to seem timeless, universal, normative, objective, rational, factual truth (Enlightenment values we still privilege):

> A faint outline known as history
> Architecture of the master builder's contribution hidden
> By the distorted mirror's take on things
> ('Meghan's Sparkle', Ronnie McGrath)

Colonialism also renders two-dimensional (and unrecognisable[8]) entire civilisations, cultures, languages, bodies of knowledge coming from outside the West: both coloniser and colonised become accustomed to 'mastering the art of being a very persistent illusion' ('MBA – Mombasa International', Nick Makoha). But the true diabolical genius of European colonialism has been to plant the ideological seeds of the dominant power's justificatory thinking into the psyches of the colonised so that they unconsciously internalise the logics of the very people who deem them to be contemptible, nonhuman or barely human.

In other words, the colonised have introjected the desire for precisely those peoples who despise and degrade them and exploit them. These psychic perversions have resulted in even their most intimate desires and their most leisurely 'tastes' to be controlled by the mad (and madness-inducing) prions of colonial thinking.

> Scrambling into a black hole
> of the mind
> Whispering like dead men
> Laughing like a poem.
>
> ('Something Moved', Hugh Stultz)

It's going to take more than Meghan Markle or a few non-white Forward Prize winners to undo this history.

What these *Filigree* poets forcefully show us is how poetry not only documents the trauma and the survival but is itself a crucial means and form not only of survival but of realising a powerful self that is not wholly captured by the nets of colonial thinking. There can be no return to an 'uncontaminated' state before colonialism, but in using the master's language, these poets show us that poetic agency can still arise from the ashes.

Their ways of resignifying English – of creating other Englishes – revivify the coloniser's language. These new forms of English are informed by nonwhite cultures outside of the UK and the United

---

8   Think of Hitler's resignification of the swastika, whose toxic afterlife saturates the world, even the 'home' culture: 'Hindu swastikas carved into geometric doors', writes Siddhartha Bose ('Polaroid, North Calcutta').

States, and they come into being from the ground up rather than primarily from university departments of English:

> Behind fingerprints
> Behind surrealism
> Behind the secret alphabet of miraculous cloud formations
> Where altars and spirits congregate to tell their stories
> In Patois and First Nation scripts
> ('Meghan's Sparkle')

And these are not poems that function as a splash of local colour, like a meal of jerk chicken or a night out at a jazz club: Echoing the great black American poet Amiri Baraka, Keith Jarrett writes, '... [Y]ou mistake my fretwork for frivolous / and fail to see the bigger loss / hidden in the smaller acts' in '(*A Black Writer Speaks of a White Woman Speaking of a Black Man Speaking of...*)'.[9]

And even when they deploy traditional forms, their poems can function as both beautiful lyric and political commentary:

> We can latch all the windows and doors
> but the sea still hears us, moves towards
> our bodies, our beds – hoarsely,
> under guidance of the moon, with green
> and white frothy arms to garland us,
> with pins to mount the beats of our lives
> against a filigreed blanket of rust.
> ('Coastal Life', Tishani Doshi)

Black British – and by this, I mean black and Asian – poets not only refuse to be silenced or erased, they actively deploy and change English-language poetics, whether by means of the inclusion of 'nonstandard' English, such as pidgin and patois, and the use of non-English languages and scripts or the techniques of fragmentation and erasure, among other formal techniques:

---

9   See Amiri Baraka/LeRoi Jones, *Blues People: Negro Music in White America* (1963; New York: HarperCollins, 1999).

Mem   oriesha   ng   lik e bird   nests
    expose   dandvi   sible
      onna k ed   bra n ches
        inwinte rair

('al zhei mer', Akila Richards)

Here, a personal familial condition (Alzheimer's) is linked to larger social and political histories and contexts: the breaking of memories and the making invisible of persons; sea trade and the ocean as a maternal ('*mer*[*e*]') womb and grave; invocations of non-Christian spirits (orishas) and non-European languages and cultures (the Arabic-sounding 'al').

These so-called Modernist techniques have largely been assumed to be beyond the provenance of nonwhite poets, who are presumed to write largely autobiographical lyrics that are either the defensive and hostile expressions of angry blackness and/or simply *cri de coeurs*.

To be sure, there are difficult painful images and subjects raised in many of these poems: there is no way not to notice the recurrence of words such as 'death', 'ash', 'ghosts', 'skin', 'white', 'fragments', 'tongue', and references to hurt, guns, war, hunger, slavery, sexual assault, loneliness, silences, mind-numbing labour – they attest to the great damage wrought and continuing to be wrought by capitalism and colonialism.[10]

Riffing off of Langston Hughes, Pete Kalu writes in 'The Negro Speaks of ~~Rivers~~ Blood Transfusions':

> I ~~bathed~~ bled out in the ~~Euphrates~~ Jim Crow time when dawns were ~~young~~ already old.

---

10   And the number of place names cited by the poets in this anthology give us an idea of the global reach of state-sponsored violence and colonial brainwashing: Mombasa, Zimbabwe, Java, the Sargasso Sea, Malacca, Calcutta, Brazil, Euphrates, Congo, Nile, Mississippi, New Orleans, Colombia, Dakar, Delhi, Sudan, Madras, Jamaica, among others.

I built my ~~hut~~ rage near the Congo and it ~~lulled~~ carried me to ~~sleep~~ war.
I looked upon the Nile and ~~raised~~ razed the ~~pyramids~~ colonials above it.
I heard the ~~singing~~ bloodbath of the Mississippi when ~~Abe Lincoln~~ Andrew Jackson
went down to ~~New Orleans~~ the slave market, and I've seen its ~~muddy~~ black bosom turn
all ~~golden~~ crimson in the sunset.

I've known ~~rivers~~ blood transfusions:
~~Ancient~~ Turbid, Oluwale ~~rivers~~ blood transfus…

In his use of strikethroughs, Kalu makes explicit the historical and material connections between the torture of slaves in the American South, the killing of David Oluwale in Leeds, and military conquests. He finds poetic solidarity and strength from the gay black American poetic genius of Hughes. And he demonstrates brilliantly that colonial history bleeds out from under the lyric lines of English poetry, whether written by a white Briton or a black American. As Kat François writes in 'Dusky Skin':

Even when silenced it [this dusky skin] speaks.
A brutalised history seeps
from its pores creeping
into an atmosphere of denial.

In keeping with the denial, most Britons and Europeans feel that colonialism was something that happened 'over there', far way in space and time, but the poet Nick Makoha reminds us that 'when I say over there I mean here' ('Bird in Flames'). Consumers in cosmopolitan first-world cities drink their cocoa, tea, rum; eat their pastries and sweets; smoke their cigars; accessorise with gold and diamonds: 'a German girl in 1st class / starts talking about the afterlife and things that belong to the dead' ('MBA – Mombasa International'). But the true cost of those 'frivolous' luxuries was paid for by blood.

Kris Manjapra reminds us that not only did '[t]he trade in slaves, and the goods they were forced to produce – sugar, tobacco and eventually cotton – create[] the first lords of modern capitalism', but '[t]he cultural legacy of slavery also infuses British tastes, from sweetened tea, to silver service, to cotton clothwork, to the endemic race and class inequalities that characterise everyday life.' He cites a graphic example of the brutality of British plantation slavery and how, while Britons back home were drinking and eating delightful fluids and solids,[11] the slaves' mouths were being filled with other things:

> …Thomas Thistlewood, a British slave owner in Jamaica in the mid-1700s … [i]n his 23 July 1756 [diary] entry…described punishing a slave in the following manner: 'Gave him a moderate whipping, pickled him well, made Hector shit in his mouth, immediately put a gag in it whilst his mouth was full and made him wear it 4 or 5 hours.'[12]

We may speak metaphorically or abstractly of slaves and people of colour having no voice but the specificity and concreteness of this act – recounted by the perpetrator in a matter-of-fact tone – speaks volumes about the literal acts of silencing that took place.[13]

Indeed, it is precisely *because of* these acts of torture and predation – not in spite of them – that white poets in England were free to pen beautiful lines of poesie. Manjapra underscores that 'Britain could not have become the most powerful economic force on earth by the turn of the 19th century without commanding the largest slave plantation economies on earth, with more than 800,000 people

11 Gin and tonics originated in colonial India as a means to mitigate the bitter taste of quinine, which was given to British soldiers as an anti-malarial.
12 Manjapra also recounts that 'Thistlewood recorded 3,852 acts of sexual intercourse with 136 enslaved women in his 37 years in Jamaica'.
13 When one considers that slave owners literally befouled and gagged the mouths, throttled and cut the throats, and lynched the necks of innumerable slaves, it is nothing short of miraculous that black poets are writing much of the best work in the English language today.

enslaved.' The enormous wealth generated by plantation slavery (what Manjapra rightly calls 'one of the greatest experiments in human terror[14] the world has ever known') not only enabled poets to write – whether those coming from country estates and Oxford and Cambridge or those poets who were not born into wealth but benefitted from the literary culture they found in cosmopolitan London and Edinburgh, glittering metropolitan centres whose wealth was fueled by slavery and empire – but the mindset and ideas and values that justified, saturated, and emanated from the practices of colonialism were part of the (white) poet's and the poems' ideas and values and poetics, too.

Indeed, more long-lasting for English poetry than colonialism's economic undergirding of poetic production is colonial racial ideology's undergirding of poetic concepts. Take, again, the poetic speaker. When we speak of a 'universal' one, do we ever imagine that speaker as black and female? And when poets – white and of colour – write for readers, whom do they imagine, consciously or not, that reader to be?

Most (white) poets and poetry scholars assume, again consciously or not, that the only poetic interiority that matters is a white interiority. Thus, the endless poems by white poets with every emotion and quotidian observation presented to the reader as if they were profound and universal truths, applicable to all humankind.

Take, too, the case of poetic tone – or that cliché-d poetry workshop idea of 'voice': Whose voice counts? And what form must poetic voice take? What tone must it strike? François writes in 'Dusky Skin',

14 While today terms such as 'terrorist', 'genocide', and 'crimes against humanity', and acts of torture rape, drug trafficking, and sociopathic behaviour are associated in the popular imaginary with ISIS, dark-skinned criminals, and newly landed nonwhite migrants, one might consider the facts and call things by their proper names, as Noam Chomsky does when he describes British '[s]tate violence . . . [as having] created by far the most extensive narcotrafficking in world history; much of India was conquered in an effort to monopolise opium production...'. Noam Chomsky, *Hopes and Prospects* (Chicago: Haymarket Books, 2010) 78.

> This dusky skin must move stealthily:
> no sudden movements which may upset
> others, tone down its voice, remove
> the bass – no reverb – so sounds exhale
> softly and ripple into nothingness.
> Its life depends on it. It must learn
> to temper its anger even when provoked [...]

This is an apt description of how a poet of colour must write in order not to upset her white reader. Talk of racism induces an extreme negative reaction in the reader by implicating her and making her feel discomfort. (At the same time, the strip-mining of white interiors has gone on for centuries so that every inch of their pain and suffering has been excavated and deemed worthy of representation.)

Yet, while things have changed somewhat for poets of colour in recent years in the UK – the awarding of poetry prizes to Vahni Capildeo, Kei Miller, and Sarah Howe, to name a few; the formation of initiatives and collectives such as The Complete Works, Octavia Collective, and RAPAPUK, among others; and the publication of anthologies of poetry by 'diverse' poets – for Black British poets who do not have Ph.D.'s or have not gone to Oxbridge or the top London universities, there is still a struggle to be heard, to find venues for publication and serious reception of their work by reviewers and scholars.

It is important that critics avoid thinking that this 'new' 'hip' prizewinning should be lauded over and above more 'identity-based' poetry written in the past or at the current moment, including (or perhaps especially) spoken-word poetry, which has had a rich and vibrant tradition in the UK. This is a false binary that we would do well to question.

What has paved the way for all nonwhite (and white) poets in Britain today has been not only generations of Black British poets – some known, some forgotten or never known; some working with collectives such as Inscribe, Cultureword, Malika's Kitchen; some on their own – but also countless Black British people, both activist and ordinary, over scores of years who have worked tirelessly at the grassroots level, in community bookstores, in private and community kitchens, on the picket line, and in untold other ways. *Filigree: Contemporary Black British Poetry* honours their legacy, their fighting spirit, their quiet determination, their persistence. The very existence of these poems were made possible by their labour:

> [...] / in this dream/ his hands trace the beginning of yours/
> reassurance that /you
> > /we are very much alive...
> > > ('Afur as Last Supper', Sumia Juxun)

But this anthology does more than show us black predecessors, poets and nonpoets, who paved the way – it puts to lie the false binaries generated by a mindset of white liberal multiculturalism and tokenism that seek to divide 'good' and 'bad' people of colour and 'good' and 'bad' poets. The unspoken rule is that 'good' poetry by people of colour may or may not include 'ethnic' elements, but it must not talk too much about or 'dwell on' the issue of race and, worst of all, racism. More 'mainstream' lyric poems might even linger on scenes of suffering but must always end on a redemptive note that does not implicate the white reader. 'Experimental' poems must either leave out racial identity completely in a cool display of abstraction or they can, again, include enough but not *too much* so as to seem leadenly gauche or to ruffle the sophisticated feathers of these white readers.

These binaries are false but have worked remarkably well to contain poets of colour and to designate which ones are worthy to be reviewed, praised, and awarded prizes. Let us not forget that, in 1756, Thistlewood used another black slave, Hector, to punish the unnamed 'bad' slave. Hector was presumably the 'good' slave for having done so. Though he was likely rewarded for his 'loyalty' to and by the master, he was much at the mercy of the colonial system and the master as was the gagged slave.

The dominance of white lyric and experimental poetry may, arguably, be on the downward slide:

> Only the earth knows why this delicate existence is a precarious
> Passage of middle and margin politics
> Of centre and decentring
> The frangible mass of it all is a delicate clock intestine whose time
>   is coming to a close
> We fade to black
>
> ('Meghan's Sparkle')

But its foundations are harder to topple. In the meantime, better to take as our models not Hector, but poems by the descendants of Hector and the unnamed slave, poems that themselves serve as testimony and powerful counter to the legacies, material and psychic, of colonialism:

> Before you silence me, know this:
>
> though headless, I'll sing.
> I'll go down in history.
>
> ('Jezebel, Guilty, Queen', Adam Lowe)

> cast them out in *Twi*, rebuke in *Fante*, loose this Pidgin to war.
>
> ('Maroon')

> On the late-night bus passing through a hostility of streets,
> I looked for mirrors – but there were none. But I began
> a testament to thinking.
> Writing. Being Here.
>
> ('Room of Mirrors', Rommi Smith)

We live in times where people are quick to jump to conclusions based on a headline without reading the article, an Instagram post with no context, a tweet barely long enough to hold the expression of a breath… My desire with *Filigree* was to find work that pretends to be frill but is ballast; headlines with the muscle of an article; Instagram posts scarred with context and tweets swollen with breath. There is a tendency in certain circles in the West, influential circles – particularly, in my experience, British literary circles, something I've spoken about publicly – to dismiss the poetry of writers of colour as being unsubtle and verbose. These dismissals and related judgements are based on a specific linguistic and musical heritage and aesthetics that while dominant should not be exclusive. Indeed, soon after the call for submissions for *Filigree* went out, there was an article in the *LA Review of Books* pre-judging the anthology before we had received the first poems. Knowing that the richness of poetry is not limited by the imaginations of critics, I made no comments in response, knowing the best riposte would be the anthology itself. And what a joy it has been to discover the fecund imagination of Black British poets of this moment.

When I chose the word 'filigree' as the title for this anthology, I was counting on its absence from regular everyday use to serve as a means of helping transcend the quotidian, of rocking the boat, of nudging writers out of their comfort zones. The idea being that at our most instinctive, we are at our most innovative and most true-to-self. It is easy, when one thinks of filigree, to fixate on the ornamental, on the notion of patterns, but, to my mind, patterns detract from the heavier truth of any object. For example, the fact that a stool is beautifully carved doesn't rob it of the ability to carry the weight of a tired woman; because a knife has an ornate pearl handle doesn't change the fact that it's an object that can kill. The aim here is to respect both the ornamentation and the function and not fall into the one-sided approach that led to the functional art of many ancient kingdoms being disdained by Western art critics who focused on the function in much the same way that contemporary literary critics can focus on the function in the work of Black poets and miss the craft. Just because something has a highly tangible function does not mean that it must lack craft – the use of the human body in dance and theatre is proof of that. The irony, of course, as art critic Jonathan Jones points out in a 2005 article in the *Guardian*, is that the idea of "art" as something *exclusively aesthetic* in nature and purpose is one of the most eccentric modern European notions, developed between the Renaissance and the 18th century. Before that, in the enlightened pre-Renaissance, poetry is craft and politics, paper and sound, experiment and logic all intertwined to create something complex, beautiful and, hopefully something that endures. Being a lover of etymology, I was also inspired by the building blocks of the word filigree, its ancestry in *filum* (thread), a thing that starts somewhere and ends somewhere else in the way that we are tied to our origins but exist elsewhere; and *granum* (seed), of the beginnings of things, the grit that begets enormity, the sand that seems to conjure itself behind an ear, weeks after your escapades on the beach. Both elements are fat with function as well as mystery.

The work that we received for *Filigree*, from both emerging and established poets, certainly rewarded my faith in the imagination of dreamers. When Victoria Adukwei Bulley speaks of 'Your voice, your vocal chords, stroked by second-hand smoke', you immediately feel an appreciation for weight, or as Tishani Doshi puts it, you sense what it might be like 'to have your neck held like a cup of wine'. There is joyful celebration of the sly in Selina Rodrigues slant rhymes for 'Jeera Sings'; in Gemma Weekes' 'The She-Mix' – a clapback at misogynist hip-hop rhymes; in the deliberate fracturing of text by Akila Richards and Rachel Long; and in the tender dismount for Raymond Antrobus' loaded 'Ode to My Hair'. Stones, sex and Siri collide here in an anthology that spans the past, to the future, the concrete to the abstract and dissects the hot topics of this epoch with a nuance that borders on the nonchalant. Two lines from Momtaza Mehri's 'Some Days, I am Too Full of Everything But Myself' come as close as one can to expressing the uncommon hybrid that *Filigree* is:

> pomegranate rind & diet lemonade boy.
> the kind of stateless i like. the kind that always finds me.

I have taken the decision not to simply have the poems under each writer's name in alphabetical order as some anthologies do because I believe it is important for readers to have an opportunity to journey through the collection. Also, freeing each poem from the need to appear in a particular place allowed me to find resonances in the work of writers who created work completely independently but were uncannily in sync. This, for me, is one of the great joys of reading this collection of poems and why everyone should read it too – it is an unaffected map of the changing face of UK poetry in all its styles. The approach is perhaps self-indulgent, but I hope that you will find pleasure in the order. Naturally, you can read *Filigree* however you want it. Ultimately, this is poetry that has faith in the logical paths that the human imagination carves out of abstraction and thus faith in the life of poetry, in the minds of its readers, the filigree it lends to any ordinary life.

Nii Ayikwei Parkes

VICTORIA ADUKWEI BULLEY

GIRL

Hair climbing down past your breasts like Jack down the beanstalk.
Your straighter teeth, your stripped upper lip (recoiling still), your
clean, dark complexion. Lean legs, or the gap between them. The
clasp of your jeans around you like a lover that you'd like to leave
– exposing the gap. The sign between your feet pointing upwards:
tear here. Sun, sea, sand and shea butter; you are smoother
skin, sanded nails, dark eyes seeing almonds. Your voice, your
vocal chords, stroked by second-hand smoke. Your dozy tongue,
stacking it over words it really should know how to shape by now.
And feet, lithe, slim – no peeling – arches secure as scaffolds.
Oiled joints, humming the silence of youth. Limbs fighting baby
jihads against lipids, still winning. Your heart still kicking it in
time, red metronome, your shunning of the night; a propensity
for restlessness, for pen against paper – a dance of sorts – because
what is death to you?

(break)

My sweet girl.

(break)

Write to me, years from today, when you no longer are what you
are now. Will you? I'd like to know what you'll be.

(break)

Call me when you find out.

(break)

I'll be here.

MOMTAZA MEHRI

SOME DAYS I AM TOO FULL OF EVERYTHING BUT MYSELF

some days this bed is so big i drown in it.
some days i fold inwards into a bag of flesh, sealed.
underneath the militarised region behind each knee,
skin soft as a plum, is a Green Zone of its own,
a slip & slide of yesterdays.

that singular lost sock under a rusting frame, bunsen-blue.
meaning i've been trying to find what used to fit,
the way i could reach under so much easier back then.
my arms got a lot bigger since, & my hands,
each palm a hollow. nah, call it a catcher's mitt

to that drowning man bopping at your throat.
a sweat bead swings from each earlobe, thicker than a blood clot.
pomegranate rind & diet lemonade boy.
the kind of stateless i like. the kind that always finds me.
hunger is each hair lifted at the nape.

or my grandfather's parietal lobe spread out in front of his home.
some kind of offering. truly, it isn't fair, yaa akhi,
it ain't. but we must have been last in line when fair was being
    handed out.
or else we'd have a belly full of something more than newspaper
    clippings.
i mean you're gonna be a headline anyway. mightaswell make a
    meal of it,

mightaswell scratch & burp & fart.
one day i'm gonna grab this horizon by its belt

but a boy named Ahmed with a freshly scraped scalp
leaning against an exit sign seems enough. for now.

& he's gonna make me fuller than a pregnant moon
or two.

RACHEL LONG

NIGHT VIGIL

I was a choir-girl. Real angel
– lightning-faced and giant for my age.

Mum let us stay up late
if we went with her to night vigil.

It started at midnight, a time too sexy to fathom;
how the minute and the hour stood to attention.

During Three Members Prayer, my sister fell asleep
under a chair, so she never knew

how I sang, or how I fell silent
when the evangelist with smiling eyes said in his pulpit voice,

Come, child.
Had she woken, I would have told her, *Sleep, sleep!*

so she'd never know Smiling Eyes
also meant teeth. Or that

he had blown candles for hands. With which
he led me down an incensed corridor,

and I followed.

TISHANI DOSHI

EVERYONE LOVES A DEAD GIRL

They arrive at parties alone because they are dead
now and there is nothing to fear except for the sun,
except for the rustle of tablecloths, which instigates
a quickening in them, the reminder of a tip-tap
phantom heart. They are beautiful, so when they stand
beside lampshades or murals, rooms shrink, and the air,
previously content to swan around in muddy shorts,
grows disgruntled and heavy. They discuss methods
of dying because even though there can be no repetition
of that experience, something about the myth of the peaceful
bed annoys them. They would like to tell people how naïve
death wishes are. They feel an exhibition of *Wounds You Never
Thought Imaginable* might help contextualise things. A girl –
call her my own, call her my lovely – stands up and says,
I would like to talk about what it means to suffocate on pillow
feathers, to have your neck held like a cup of wine, all delicate
and beloved, before it is crushed. Another stands, and another,
and even though they have no names and some of them
have satin strips instead of faces, they all have stories
which go on and on – ocean-like, glamorous – until
it is morning and they go wherever it is dead girls go.

In the parties of the real world people talk about how some
girls walk down the wrong roads and fall down rabbit holes.
People who haven't put their faces in the soft stomach
of another's for years, who no longer go out at night
to chase the moon. Even those people who do nothing
but make love in grass all day long. Benevolent people.
Their hearts leap when they hear a story of a dead girl,
and when they tell it to someone (how could they not?)
the telling is a kind of nourishing – all the dormant bits
inside them charge around like Bolshoi dancers re-entering

the world, alive and with wonder. Because how could you not
hold on to your wrists and listen to *that that that*
unquestionable bloom? How could you not fall apart
with relief? And when they hold their own girls close,
maybe they tell them how beauty is a distance
they don't need to travel. Maybe they construct braids
from their chestnut hair and, while doing this, imagine
they are trees. Truly, they believe themselves when they say,
the world is a forest, darling, remember the bread crumbs,
remember to dig a tunnel home through the rain.

LOUISA ADJOA PARKER

THE JEWELLERY MAKER

Each day after sunrise he walks to the workshop
– like his father before him, and his father too –
the slap of sandalled feet on heat-baked stone,
the smell of blossom, a plate-blue sky. He greets
his neighbours with a smile. In the distance
a wild dog barks.

He sits straight-backed, lays out pointed tools
the way a surgeon might – neat as soldiers.
He likes hot metal, the smell, the way it yields
to his touch. Under deft fingers gold butterflies dance;
flowers bloom; silvery moons wax and wane,
then wax again; bright dragonflies flap two pairs of wings.

He likes the tiny loops and curls – he'd decorate
his house in this, drape his wife in fine-spun gold;
her skin wrinkled by sun, in simple cotton dress,
her only jewellery a plain gold band, worn thin.
He imagines the women who will wear
what he has made, clear-eyed, bird-boned, unlined skin
warming the metal his hands caress.

NICK MAKOHA

MBA – MOMBASA INTERNATIONAL

Minutes after the Airbus takes off, a German girl in 1st class
starts talking about the afterlife and things that belong to the dead.

One man swallows duty-free rum to replace the taste of sugarcane,
his skin hissing and spitting like a fuse as the sun glides in reverse.

He is mastering the art of being a very persistent illusion.
This is mine: *the world is connected by a circle.*

*The same circle a man might make folding his arms around
another man's shoulder.* Light bends through the cabin.

At the edge of my window small towns pass.
Clouds cascade and dance.

We are both holding our breath reciting the laws of probability.
My eyes are closed. I call it the garden of the blind.

I am back in the old world where light bends through the clouds.
The soldier by the kiosk loves the taste of his words.

Women jostle for provisions. Their children wade ankle deep
in water. Their reflections dance across the surface.

Two continents away a cameraman lifts his hand for silence
in the oil refinery that looks bigger than he imagined.

Two men walk in the dark. The camera lens searching
for the quality of lost light. They are moving by memory

of a stolen blueprint tattooed on their minds.
I have the same tattoo.

SENI SENEVIRATNE

BECAUSE HE LOVED LETTERS

and the opening of them, I gave it to him,
though it seemed to have been always his.

Its handle is carved into the head and wings
of a bateleur eagle, Shona bird of good fortune,

with eyes of bone. A keepsake from the ruins
of Great Zimbabwe where, ten centuries ago,

the Gokemere made towers of rock, climbing
as they built, dropping rope and stone for plumblines.

I'd say the wood is mahogany but for the flash of
honeyed grain on one wing and the very tip of its beak.

It has come back to me now, though it was also
always with me and lives in my blue ceramic pen-jar.

Sometimes I take it out, for the feel of its sharp edge
against my lips, the taste of questions never asked.

ZENA EDWARDS

RESISTANCE IS FERTILE

Winds of love's season
her hair's breath swept the nape of his neck.
The dulled mountains of him shuddered;
her gentleness spoke to the crags
in the croaks of his denials.
Fissures in the grey face of his loneliness filled
with sweet figments of promises – she sat beside him. Real.

Fragile bud
the earth of her fed blossoms he would have ignored
if she were not holding his hand under the table.
He always thought the skeletons of petals
were too fragile, yet the lines on his palm
fed the flower of his hand unfurling
then vining his fingers around hers.

Watering can
he'd said he had no patience for the weight of dew:
'Either rain or don't.' Now
his hand cupped
the fine mists that curled
around her waist.
His resistance, fertile, softened under the water of her gaze.

Her insistent conflagration
cracked – the silver ash coating his blackened skin
a map of the embers still simmering beneath,
after moon-licked love-making flared the midsummer night.
Body, once taut from several winters of duplicity,
thawed, spilling through the weft of cream cotton sheeting,
the cilia of his frayed edges sweeping him to harbour in her arms.

FAWZIA KANE

CINNAMON

Watch how the skin peels, dislodges, is
sloughed off to reveal layers of mottling, so
soft and moist. It holds a tint only burning
sugar can show, at that instant when it
granulates from smooth clay to sheets of
beaten copper. This wound, just here on
the trunk, has already dried. Even the leaves
turn brittle, curl into fingers, and desiccate
to crumbs. Examine these differences of
duskiness, the scale of halftones that play
out among and over us, during our quick
dawns and lingering twilights. How many
will mingle in crowds, to be tied to others
with strings of painted lines? Which of
these, when they touch and interweave
with us, will you still believe are invisible?
Remember, remember the splintering of
their scent through the prism of air, the lick
of it, the hot taste against the inside of our
throats, the hurt on, the hurt of the tongue.

MICHAEL CAMPBELL

SECRET PLACE

into the wilderness of a clutter –
of unopened bills, a noiseless clatter
of six-winged seraphim, worn-in
Nike Air Force Ones, brogues, slippers,
piled against the wardrobe.
into the exile of pages,
unread columns of books, DC Comics,
the voice of God comes like the want
of bread, an urge of hunger that makes
you lie down on an empty belly
to quiet the stomach.
into a pilgrimage of tears,
an altar by the bed, a washing of
the master's feet on the firmament
of a footstool. in this place made with words
are delicate kisses, intricate whispers
that only the eyes speak.
eyes that have seen things and with their salt
preserve something of that light.

SAI MURRAY

CORAL

you have an eye for glass. an eye, the breath, the hand.
kick, kicking against gentle surf, you steady yourself.
hover. pounce.

after each punch, you raise a fist in victory,
let the sand-cloud stream through fingers
revealing the nugget.

you grade the catch from rare azure to common brown.
opal, green, clear and terracotta gems in between.
the ocean's smithery judged on smoothness, and curve.

the coral never held your interest:
too sharp, too knobbly for swim-short pockets.
too bulky, too brittle for the suitcase.

but then, far far from your beach
in a cold pale village, in a shop window,
you find a sea fan. captured, locked in a frame.

a handwritten label names your island
and speaks a price
many times the cost of a hot meal.

bells and shells sound as you try the door.
you think of thrashing, churning waves.
smashing glass. recycling. reframing.

returning to the sea.

LYNNE E. BLACKWOOD

YEKATERINABURG

I nestled
in your petticoat
folds snug amidst the silken
underskirts where all your wealth
was sewn. I lay beside a bird brooch, an
emerald peacock whose inset diamond eyes
lie lifeless against lacklustre sapphire cheeks.
No plush velvet to cushion us but worn silk taffeta
stuffed with bedraggled eiderdown soiled by Siberian
mud over those open prison months. This is no swallow
nest,
enclosed, secure, but a hidden cage devoid of songbirds.
Fabergé spun gold around my ivory egg, embellished
me with the brilliance of jewels. We were your past
and hopeless future, Anastasia, your nest egg
clung heavy around juvenile ankles
until felled in one swoop
by comrades'
bullets.

ADAM LOWE

BOY-MACHINE

I.
Last night I dreamed of Icarus
stitching wings of silk and feather
on wax. He stretched the thatch
over a lightweight wooden frame,
the way a lover's embrace covers
a starved man with flesh. Last night
I fevered with thoughts of him.
tasted his buttocks' dark cleft,
felt the swim of saltwater sweat
down his spread limbs, flew closer.

II.
In his workshop: Leonardo
dreams of a boy-machine lifted,
held up against the sky

to wink like chiselled flint,
a specimen jewel. Leonardo
imagines a world that moves

without hands. He conjures
up wheels that spin kingdoms.
Leonardo is in love.

III.
I bolt the wings to my forearms:
blades collected from helicopters,
edging like rotary petals.

I thread wire along the length
of my veins, fire muscle
with electricity, lightning from

cumulonimbus gods. I am a spark
ready to fly. I climb upon
the cottage roof, wings poised

like a weather vane; stare
past twilight and molten wax,
the threat of falling. Rocket man,

missile, scissor-bird, I launch
for space, I score the clouds,
through oceanic skies, weightless.

SELINA RODRIGUES

FARROKH

Farrokh sweeps water into water.
      Night is always awake – a single bark,
      gin-soaked refrains and under the low lights
         the pool is deeper than it is.

Criss-cross of tiles, he closes umbrellas.
      He knows heat, its slow changes.
      An ice-dancer glides on the 24-hr screen
         and guns raise dust and sand.

In another hotel, another calls.
      Farrokh's eyes close, his body played
      like piano keys, dizzy as children
         who clasp hands and spin.

Somewhere spotlit, his shoulders are bare.
      He catches the falling notes of
      a man on his tongue.
         Somewhere rain falls for days,

certain as the kiss of young people held
      amongst young people. Oh Freddie sings,
      pure as a spring. Farrokh knows his future
         close to him as a second skin.

NANDITA GHOSE

FLIGHT

The birds fly east
wings unflayed
by the sun.

I stand by Time,
her hands unchained
her hair hangs down,
mud on her lips.

And mine move
silently and ceaselessly,
'Let me go with the birds,
for the sky reigns all,
engulfs the stars and ships, shrouds the ash rising from the pyre.
Let me rise with the birds.'

One tear from her eye
glides to earth
as silently and ceaselessly
she whispers no.

Now only flight's
breath remains.

NICK MAKOHA

BIRD IN FLAMES

A man and his beer talk to another man; after a swig from a dark bottle his lips leak out a *Hmmm*. In the first death, I am a bird darting from an oncoming pick-up truck under starlight, as I head for the grass. A static quiet; the pick-up drives down the road. Two men mention genocide, a third struggles to confess that he has spoken to the tribes and it stirred conflict.

Earlier, the third man was blindfolded: a hand rests at the bottleneck of his throat, a knife at his wrists. Others surround him under a low purple light. Discomfort drips from his mouth. They are looking for a reaction. The moment is disguised as a get-together, hence the beer, meat and chapattis and women's voices outside, rising over music.

The third man's arms are crossed as a deep voice enters the discussion and asks, *Truthfully, Bishop, where are the arms?* The night has an Indian heat; silence glues the third man to his seat. The Voice has set a table. He leans into the Bishop's ear, rolls his sleeve and invites him to join, once he has told him where the guns are. *The guns! The guns.*

The Bishop replies, *I can exist without your formality, without these courtesies. What meal have you prepared that I have not eaten?* The Voice kicks his chair out from under him. Back in the pick-up the bodies are not moving; no side glances. They pass a school, a settlement, a store, a trading post in the hills… but there is no conversation.

Notice the bird, the car's headlights like fireflies. Since the moment has passed I can tell you there was no bird, but the men were real, and the chair with its table full of food. The only thing missing are the bullets. A second death. That is how nations die over there. When I say nation I mean tribes; when I say tribe I mean people, when I say over there I mean here.

FAWZIA KANE

HERETIC
(after Dante, redacted)

    the squall sent
a sound   one that ripped
along the dust   before
making   beasts   run   for shelter

while
       your eyes fix where
       the smoke is thickest

while

a thousand ruined   scatter away
and wait for   some messenger to sign away   **silence!**

what scorn there   is for outcasts

    why do you   set yourselves   against your own rebellion
close   your   open gates   learning nothing
but itch to laugh at those who burn

            while

 a city with a river   will still   sink into stagnant marshes
in a country bounded by a sea   whose waters
   wash   uneven tombs
buried in a ring   with lids upraised   un-

ending   and between

CHRISTINA FONTHES

HOW TO WRAP A *LIPUTA* WHEN MAKING LOVE
TO A MARRIED MAN

Mothers and aunties would rarely admit,
but making love to a married man
is an art we excel in.

On the night, wear the red and gold one
with the Euro and Dollar print.
Red, for seduction.
Gold, so that he remembers your school fees.
Ensure that it hangs loose

and that he is well-hung.

Do not expose all of you:
Breasts   yes.

Legs   yes.

Cover up: birthmarks, tattoos, scars
– physical and non-physical.
If not, when he is angered by things that have
nothing to do with you,
he will use these marks
to shame you.

Hold him, to the point of suffocation
leave no room for breath
or guilt.
When your limbs become exhausted,
use the selvedge to dab beads of sweat off his chest.

When, at 2am, you awake
eyes   searching
for his laced *Westons* behind the door
you will inhale him –
the balm for your wounds.

You will find a roll on the bedside table.
Dollar bills. Carelessly tossed
between the Gideon Bible
and the late-night service menu.

RACHEL LONG

THE ART OF UNDRESSING

ake down the clock
urn over your pho
he only thing that sho
ibrate in thi
lace, you want somethi
reathable, something you
an remove easily; think
   otton
   ilk   ockings
ribb
      orset
the reparation is eve
 immer   your clavi
 row bone
 ulbs of should
shins an flour
  ude toes. Gold
 arobes, ongue of
  owing this time to
 illow hair, a bow
 or ring
pla e your fin ers on
the purpl eathers. Si
 eve it to the floo
eye con   is ever ing

RISHI DASTIDAR

PLUCK

Swept her into the nearest bed?
Scalpel down the sweetheart neckline,
open up the red gingham dress
and once you've got past the undercoat
of knots you will find her pluck.
It might be corroded by the smokes
and the cocktails, but this is not the time
for timidity, let alone veneration or superstition.
Here is your work then:
using sharp eyes, soft ears and kind words
reach in and make sure that
the world has room to play.
Have one last whisky, one later kiss
and remember: love lies down every day.

ADAM LOWE

JEZEBEL, GUILTY, QUEEN

You call me Jezebel: temptress, false idol
in shallow spotlight, pedlar of blasphemy and unnatural sex.

You call me unsuited, shock slut of back alleys,
siren seed-spilling in the thrashing of night.

You call me a queen. Paint me Anne Boleyn.
Paste on my make-up,
sharp-set and glittering.

These pearls I clutch as sexy rosaries.
Before you silence me, know this:

though headless, I'll sing.
I'll go down in history.

RUTH SUTOYÉ

PRAISE SONG

(FOR)   womyn   with eyes hollow & tree trunk back
             womxn   who soak battle in laughter oil
             womxn   practising softness on each other
             womxn   who've stopped offering body as atonement
             womxn   who still offer body as communion
             womxn   with superpower to hear breaking souls
             womxn   onyx skinned   marking bravery up the
                             walls of each other's thighs
                             as if tomorrow's breath is Bermuda Triangle
             womxn   making refugee camps of each other, dragging
                             memories over barbed wire
(FOR)   womxn   who love men that ruin them
             womxn   who perdure men that ruin(ed) them
             womxn   with time bombs for fathers
             womxn   with bitter wombs   where generations choke
             womxn   from mothers with no language
             womxn   whom we forgot *(forgive us)*
             womxn   handing down trauma as heirloom
             womxn   the colour of fear, sprinting barefoot to godknows
                             but they were taught to run
             womxn   who cross-stitch tapestries on
                             their lover's collarbone
                             sewing kisses only in bluest dark
                             because sunrise comes with crucifixion
(FOR)   womxn   serving as poster models for agony
             womxn   running out of time
             womxn   who are placard and protest and rockstone
             womxn   desperate for 16 piece orchestra love, fatigued
                             from the caesarean kind
(FOR)   womxn   who smear the blood of their firstborns
                             across their homes praying the angel of death
                             will pass them by

woman who love womxn who love womyn
who love women
*let us practice softness together**

(*After Malika Booker & Caleb Femi)

RACHEL LONG

SMOULDER

Smoke your face through silk.
The thumbskin weave
this close. Look
through the burn hole.
Knickers smoulder in the ashtray.
A train coming. Tearing through
an old country station.
Or between the legs
of a living room. Or old bedroom.
But there is no house attached,
no destination – just a door,
wide open and vacant
as a window.

CHRISTINA FONTHES

AT THE *MATANGA* – ANY *LIPUTA* WILL DO

Your Grandmother's old *Super Wax*
still carrying the faded face of Mobuto.
The kind that can only be found decorating

the hips of *Big Ladies* – wives of important men.
The worn Java that you received
on your tenth birthday

brown and blue.
A Chinese imitation
fit for a girl who has not yet bled.

Wrap it around your waist, like the jobless
husbands that sit indoors
ashamed.

Drape it over your shoulders
the edges will hang dejectedly
in perfect reach for mourners

to dab your tears.
The tired cloth may wish
to escape your beating breast

to seek refuge on the floor.
Let it.
Expose all of you.

In mourning, even first wives do not judge.

TOLU AGBELUSI

FAKING DEATH TO AVOID SEX IS NOT EXTREME

Death is a mating ritual
– the base of my wings bitten off
by a male seizing my body
mid-flight. It's a vice
with spiny claspers from a dragon hunter
who insists I lay my eggs before he leaves
– one who doesn't care that his iron hold
gouges my eyes, pierces my head
and splits my exoskeleton.

This is a death I can come back from.
You know this. You know how it feels
to make a corpse of your body, hoping
the one you thought you knew notices,
vacates his excitement and ceases pursuit.
You know the silence. How it crowds
your breathing for days after. The pondering
over what else you could have done.
The extra layers cladding your skin
as you try to disappear in broad daylight.

Is this not what sister damselfly does
when she forces the evolution
of her green stripes blue to mimic
the males? Trick them
away from harassment
if only for a while. Is this not
how we practise being strong?
Breaking ourselves in pieces
so we can choose the one
fragment that stays whole.

MAGGIE HARRIS

VOYAGE IN THE DARK
(*For Hilary*)

We swim towards each other in the dark.
An oily dark, buoyed by tentacles of memory
that brush past our ears like feathers. Inconstant
syllables linger, phrases regroup and reform;
your turquoise earrings swing in their film
of silver against your cheek.

Your eyes float towards me in the gloom.
Elizabeth Taylor eyes, they once danced with mirth
and innuendo, head tipped back for another glug
of wine, poetry tossed with pancakes
and metaphors mixed as salads.

You can no longer make tea. Your kitchen
is a place of unfamiliar things you wander
with lost hands. We are marooned here.
Seamus Heaney is still in the shed. Plath
and Hughes drop in, revitalise
our meetings as they always do, shine
a light on our constant tussle with ideas and form.
Sometimes Walcott returns, like the *Wide Sargasso Sea,*
Sugar and Slate, 'that lovely Charlotte', me,
those you welcomed with open palms.
I stroke the vein-blue thin of your hands,
From far away the clock booms
another hour.

AKILA RICHARDS

AL ZHEI MER

Mem   oriesha   ng   lik e bird   nests
expose   dandvi   sible
onna k ed   bra n ches
inwinte rair

Oldcon   struc t i on of   drie dup   t wigs
feathersand   bro   ken   s hell s
c   lingsto   crac ks   crad lesof
em   ptiness.

DEGNA STONE

THE HOUSE THROWN OUT BY HER VILLAGE

The house thrown out by her village sits isolated in a patch of abandoned ground, her windows glaucomaed with grime. Her floors and ceilings have crumbled, taking away the definition of rooms. She is all space. If you can take the danger of not knowing where to put your feet she'll welcome you in with an open door. There is a lack. A missing. A want. She is breaking down, has broken down, but despite being alone for so long she has not grown tired of herself. Listen hard and keep a sense of where everything used to be. And where your room could have been.

INDIGO WILLIAMS

THE GARDEN IS BARE

Because I cannot manage
the heft and ache
of your garden by myself
I pulled out the white lilies
with the weeds,
threw away the plant pots
and the random beer cans
the drunk nights tossed in.
The cherry tree is taller
than the house now
but I don't know how
to keep the maggots
from eating your fruit.
I uprooted your apple tree
and I swear it wept or maybe
something in me wept
when its branches snapped
like dry bones. I pulled it out
by its roots but some of it
grew back and like me,
it keeps on living.

MAYA CHOWDHRY

TERMINAL BUD

Upturned my many eyes
view treetops arrow-like
towards the sun. My sap
is severed,
disconnected I dangle, fall.

The place where I connected
to tree is shrivelled, dried shut.
I despair as my seed faces
stare at you wondering
when more of me will open.

I am a fountain of forgetting,
scent of forest floor.
Compared to dandelion
I am dead.

You grip this death,
looking for comparisons, after
the indents on your fingers
fade to smooth skin.

You pluck my cone scale,
making music of me. A mini
marimba calling the pine warbler
to roost. After your melody
I turn myself back, to nature.

TISHANI DOSHI

COASTAL LIFE

It takes years of coastal living to understand
that you are the lifeless Malacca snake
discarded from the fisherman's net,
buried in sand. That you are connected
to the million ephemera wings, clogging
the balcony drains. That seasons will bring
rotting carapace of turtle, decapitated
tree frogs, acres of slain mosquitoes.
All night the electricity surges and stops,
smothering wires and fuses, while lizards
plop. The resident mouse leaves imprints
of his teeth in banana skins, knowing
that soon, quite soon, he will succumb
to the poisoned biscuits we lay out for him.
Underground, roots of bougainvillea
delicately throttle the water pipes,
and as if sensing this menace, the dogs,
uneasy in sleep, move their frantic legs
against concrete in pursuit of a chicken.
Even the door-jambs, plump with rain,
know that something is coming to prise
open our caskets, unhinge us with salt.
We can latch all the windows and doors
but the sea still hears us, moves towards
our bodies, our beds – hoarsely,
under guidance of the moon, with green
and white frothy arms to garland us,
with pins to mount the beasts of our lives
against a filigreed blanket of rust.

HUGH STULTZ

SOMETHING MOVED

Something moved
In the bushes
Under a blanket of dead leaves
Under the dust

Something shaped like smoke
Sudden as lightning
Flashed past
I
Groping, touched something
Wet like morning
Soft as baby flesh
Darting between the splintered sunlight
Scrambling into a black hole
of the mind
Whispering like dead men
Laughing like a poem.

KEISHA THOMPSON

GÖKOTTA

Given space and light, a dusty patch
on the ground will wait to be treated
like a dance floor again; a rippling skirt
can emboss the edges of a melody.

She removes her shoes, pinches her skirt
hems. She doesn't know the meaning
of the lyrics and they don't know the meaning
of her; still there is conversation.

KAT FRANÇOIS

DUSKY SKIN

This dusky skin cannot hide, cannot
blend into the background.
Even when silenced it speaks.
A brutalised history seeps
from its pores creeping
into an atmosphere of denial.
It must master how to sit
when others stand, stand when others sit,
mould itself into whatever shape,
society demands.

This dusky skin must move stealthily:
no sudden movements which may upset
others, tone down its voice, remove
the bass – no reverb – so sounds exhale
softly and ripple into nothingness.
Its life depends on it. It must learn
to temper its anger even when provoked,
to smile in the face of its oppressor.
It must not show its true nature.
It must always appear to conform.

This dusky skin must master blandness,
merge into grey, water itself down, squeeze itself
into the tiniest space possible. Blend, blend,
it must learn to blend, become less visible,
less aggressive, less provoking, less threatening...
Bend, contort, manipulate, twist, turn,
this dusky skin must learn to survive.

MOMTAZA MEHRI

REPEAT AFTER WE

a sunbreak writes on our backs / reminds us we are not her children / laughs at a diaspora's SPF factors / their daily self-delusions / we are bathed in white / a shawl of light around our necks /

we are pooled necessity / liquid hanging from earlobes / from the meat of wrists / there is no name for this /

only us attached by the fingertips / to this day & every day before it / before us / we are walking full circles /

a skybreak is a gash in the knee / a plane's womb / looking above is the same in all accents /

no-one makes fun of baaba here / falling is universal / i took a photo of the landing step / bleached altar /

its gangplank promises / linearity as luxury / between the breach of my thighs / a camera stands witness /

stands in my place / i am still processing / where the light never reaches /

a heavenbreak is inevitable / us who can only find Him in dead currency / run to the money transfer /

to translate it / into a lush of franklins / a fistful of ulysses / or something else sanctified / something we can barter for time / for another night free of guilt's rough tongue / we send what we can / to forget / what we can / they are over there / i am here / this isn't anyone's fault / fate's arithmetic has no favourites /

i promise i will visit again / sometime soon / i promise i will be content / with not being needed / with being useless / i will search for your scent / blame no one / if i do not recognize it /

DEGNA STONE

PERFIDIA

It's like listening to Siri navigate
after his voice changed in the update.

You know what he's saying
but not what he's getting at.

It's his diction. Clipped. Like
he's withholding something from you.

How can you trust him?
You want to see the shape of his mouth,

watch the words physically form
on the lips he doesn't have.

How can you understand what he's saying
if you can't *see* what he's saying?

Instead, his words appear by magic.
And who can understand magic?

MAYA CHOWDHRY

OPTIONS

> root stock chopped
> taste another minute
> remaining tender (optional)

You've genetically engineered a blue
orchid – and? An orchid can evolve past
blue. Profit will grow humans with two
sheep heads; but then there will be more
mouths to feed.

> dilated occidental svelte
> (Hooker f.) *Soo*: ground
> hitherto unknown, given

In the catalogue you type f. = female but
chromosomely she has no ovules. You
have assigned her nonetheless.

KEITH JARRETT

(*A BLACK WRITER SPEAKS OF A WHITE WOMAN SPEAKING OF A*
BLACK MAN SPEAKING OF...)

If it were just two people
the whole ting wouldda easy

like the couple who toe-dip by
Black River under different shades

though could be out of many shades
of a different sun whose cast dictates

whose story it is to tell or could be
it is none of their stories or just none   of my business.
*
Or if I could tell this a different way you cannot
read my face exactly the way I am writing it even
if I practice holding myself in the mirror everything
is inverted
*
Or if I could tell this another way again:
I am sitting at a crossroads/ wrestling with fresh blood /
in a new principality /and you mistake my fretwork for frivolous /
and fail to see the bigger loss/ hidden in the smaller acts.
*
Mi mean seh everyting does invertation
& many things teg tsol: the erutcip reggib
the blood road sitting; how we talk about shadows
Caste   Cast   Cas   Ca   C   c
*
The Black River makes way for two toe-Moseses
then folds over itself again   rolls its eyes

71

for when they speak of water over bridges
it is precisely this: the white foam & the black

depths pressing and pressing & relentless
in-betweening of chewing gum wrappers

and Styrofoam. The day you drink of it
you will surely (whose snake was it anyway?) die.

RONNIE MCGRATH

MEGHAN'S SPARKLE

A faint outline known as history
   Architecture of the master builder's contribution hidden
          By the distorted mirror's take on things
The subtle moon bears witness to the pyramid's unfolding
       Incredible leaves of an expanding edifice that it is
The Nubian sky knows the wisdom of stars when awoken
  Their Jimmy Baldwin eyes looking for the mystery of me
               Behind fingerprints
               Behind surrealism
Behind the secret alphabet of miraculous cloud formations
  Where altars and spirits congregate to tell their stories
          In Patois and First Nation scripts

Slice by slice I am imaged wrong in the calculated effect of a hit movie
  Bleached out of the nude sunlight by the cartographers realignment
My pharaoh's nose without landmass or shore to cling to

  Only the earth knows why this delicate existence is a precarious
Passage of middle and margin politics
Of centre and decentring
The frangible mass of it all is a delicate clock intestine whose time
  is coming to a close
We fade to black
Safe in the roots of our melaskin
    E-raced.

SIDDHARTHA BOSE

POLAROID, NORTH CALCUTTA

Winding lane, green limestone wash.
Red flowers – sickles, hammers –
patched onto peeling walls.

Hindu swastikas carved into geometric doors.
Three bony canines, lazing, like the city,
ragged and potholed.

Woman – hair covered, white cloth,
dusts a chessboard.

Each little house, a different shade, different
colour.
~~

Three boys play cricket,
upturned red bricks as wickets.

They break away, seeing strangers.

One, shirt tucked tight in-
to dark brown shorts,

black hair oiled in a side parting,
sticks out his hand, for shaking.

(my hands are wet in the afternoon sun)

~~

The lane blooms to a small piazza.
A tree, two benches, crowded with men.

A shop with broken, electronic spare parts.
The boss wears a monkey cap, jeans,
red shawl, black shades.

A carcass of an old van, eyeless.
~ ~

Girls in fanned skirts hopscotch. Boys
toss coins, watch them fall and clatter,
rusted and shining,

dying suns.

A family of three children,
ragged vests, surround blank noise.

The noise is the combustion of
falling satellites.

They part, revealing –
in a cave – a cage of birds.

Parrots, mynas, koels.
Alien specimens from Brazil, the children say.
~ ~

The cage howls in the middle of this circle.
The noise tumbles into the tattered, oil-slicked sack of the city.

The sky burns yellow.

PATRICIA FOSTER McKENLEY

BENCH, RELLEU, ALICANTE

Where she sits, each of her tired vertebrae
rests against delicate latticework

of spirals and question mark curves,
on a black wrought-iron bench,

on this narrow, slanting Alicante Street.
She shuffles, shifts back, her neck cradle

uncomfortable on the dip in the top curve
of the bench. Leans forward, sits upright

and can see the distant Alicante hills
are black ink water-washes and smudged

charcoal in quaint spots. To passers by,
she is one of Picasso's *Les Demoiselles d'Avignon,*

with her distorted nose, morose jet black
African eyes; a curio, no smile, confined within

peripheries of intricate lines of brush strokes,
against white canvas. A lone car engine's moaning

first gear pulls a dusty red Citroën, up and around
the winding street,

where its driver and three other olive-skinned
faces, in unison, turn her way. The street sprouts

mango sorbet houses with wooden shutters
and pastel coloured blinds pulled by peeping hands,

and balconies, with benches
like the one she sits on. She watches the Citroën

now reverse back down the incline, ignoring
a bold blue one-way sign

with compromising white arrow. Here,
the days are sleepy and their dates overlap.

Leans back on spiralled ribs of black iron
where the latticed wire works are warm

to touch from the 3pm bleached-white sun.
She wonders if staring passers by –

like the man with his weather-beaten face
and ruddy cheeks – will at last form

their frozen open mouths to say *Hola,
buenas tardes* to a Picasso painting.

IONEY SMALLHORNE

SPINNERET

She stores memories
as silk in glands
deep within her abdomen

the eighth leg sprouted after
the murder of her son
she is now a spider

and weaves a lace fortress
one thread for her first born Maliki
she is solitary and black

one thread for the smell of Rocky's fish market
webbing an almanac
one thread for the uncle that crushed her

she is dextrous and exact
one thread for picking mangoes with Lyn
she's forever in her zodiac

weaving breaking repairing
her life patterned, knotted
like macrame

PETE KALU

THE NEGRO SPEAKS OF ~~RIVERS~~ BLOOD TRANSFUSIONS
(*After Langston Hughes*)

I've known ~~rivers~~blood transfusions:
I've known ~~rivers~~ blood transfusions ancient as ~~the world~~ my soul
and older than the
flow of ~~human blood~~ rivers in ~~human~~ earth's veins.

My ~~soul~~ pulse has grown ~~deep~~ slow like the rivers.

I ~~bathed~~ bled out in the ~~Euphrates~~ Jim Crow time when dawns
were ~~young~~ already old.
I built my ~~hut~~ rage near the Congo and it ~~lulled~~ carried me to
~~sleep~~ war.
I looked upon the Nile and ~~raised~~ razed the ~~pyramids~~ colonials
above it.
I heard the ~~singing~~ bloodbath of the Mississippi when ~~Abe
Lincoln~~ Andrew Jackson
went down to ~~New Orleans~~ the slave market, and I've seen its
~~muddy~~ black bosom turn
all ~~golden~~ crimson in the sunset.

I've known ~~rivers~~ blood transfusions:
~~Ancient~~ Turbid, Oluwale ~~rivers~~ blood transfus...

My soul has grown ~~deep~~ red like the ~~rivers~~ blood transf

JOSHUA IDEHEN

GRENFELL

Living   in
LDN   is
a   hard
ship. Little
choice but
to   shuffle
into   a
match stick

GEMMA WEEKES

THE SHE-MIX
(*For Hip-Hop and your Mum*)

Bitches baretitted – (dance) twerk/grin – red throats open –
gaping – into dead poison silence – these walls
Aint good for nothing – but sweat/forgetting/violence – (switch
mind off) – these bitches is bookends – he the
Shit – the dookie – girls wanna do/screw – (Who? You?) – blank-
headed – vacuum – dance
But don't *move* – these words have teeth – (I) struggle – torn
double – in the jaw of the groove – where we're all
Hoes – hollowed down to the meat – #yesallwomen – (me.) –
tableau steeped in shadow – mouthless roar
And slick flows – weaving bravado into – individual prisons – (are
we all victims?) – the beat
Tricks us into sleeping – (I) I! startle from imposed dreams into
swallowed scream – these bitches is me - these

Bitches – distilled from full-blooded planets – (held down/f**kd)
– intricate as pomegranates – I
Ain't ask for this – (spread wide) – being the despised/prized
opposite – this vagina gave birth to time – no
Shit – nothing without it – (no!)/thing and no/one – including
you – including your tongue – wake up - broken
But alive – indelible – stunned (gone) – music stripped naked –
revealed as diseased to the bone – making
Hoes of magicians – slaves of our mothers – tomb of the future –
dead fossils of all potential
And with every record sold – a free soul – hollowed down to the
meat – the plugged crown
Tricks slipshod feet – we go sleep in the beat – I wake up in
mourning – that good – clear – cold

('Bitches' like me
Ain't taking that
Shit – think yourself a pimp wrapped in dead skin and heavy
    chains
But a pimp ain't pawned at his own game – the only real
Hoes trade self-belief for make believe, rolling over for bankrolls
And one day it will cost too much to keep your head closed cuz
    these
Tricks ain't free.)

MICHAEL CAMPBELL

MAROON

'You taught me language, and my profit on't
Is I know how to curse.' Shakespeare, *The Tempest*

cast them out in *Twi*, rebuke in *Fante*, loose this Pidgin to war.
think man *mad* blood? think water. think bloodied masthead,
dragoon spirit come over, carry legion. run man aground. That
same windswept squall

will try wrap-up the isle of the head & gallop like worms in
turned pork but I squat in there, shoot me one from the saddle.
batten shipwrecked words together. make *good* bad-talk, piece-
piece makeshift brass gun,

gift a plug o' bullets to smoke out the Marlborough men.
bawl burning huts from blue-bearded hillsides. watch colonial
catechisms squirm in the rage of discontented cloves of red. I eat
literature alive. have ravaged to the page

the flesh of *Tennyson* and revisited it – a dog to its vomit. my
head no good, empires are crumbling on my saurian spines. I,
Caliban with a skin fade: Babel's wreckage pieced together am all
reclaimed land. imagine, it took

53 shiploads of dirt from Calvary to prop up the bell tower
at Pisa. just think, the belfry sits in some litter carried by
subservient soil that soaked the blood of thieves, slaves,
insurrectionists, innocents, the firstborn of us. always

an empire somewhere wants to ride my shoulders. wants to
mount my back. wound man's spirit, break man in. I carry
people in mine. a wrath of words, a scatter of unknown tongues
& know that the Babel of their empire is a feeble leaning tower.

SELINA NWULU

DEPARTES*

A woman sits under a Colombian mahogany tree
plaiting a girl's hair. Her Afro is lush forest,
a congregation of dense prayers, tall defiance
amidst days of backbreak and whiplash.
See how quick calloused hands know how to whisper
escape into scalp, grease direction into braids.
To take three strands, weaving the left over right
under middle, left right middle, left right middle
with surgeon dexterity. A central braid
starting at the peak of the skull: *Do not stray too far
from the river.* A twisted offshoot to the left:
You will hear the thunder of Spanish boots.
Wait, do not let your breath intrude their depravity.
A zigzag parting: *Do not take a right turn here
for there is nothing but the skeletons of the fallen.*
Two braids intertwined: *Cross the bridge and run,
my loves, run towards the top of the mountain.*

And how my own mother plaited my hair
every young Sunday, tresses interlocked
across centuries and continents. Pot of Sulfur8
in my hand, head leaning on the inside of her thigh.
She too wove into my scalp the words she could not say,
took three strands of hair weaving the left over right
under middle, left right middle, left right middle,
with surgeon dexterity. A central braid
starting at the peak of the skull: *I plait for you
a crown, because you will not always be thought of as queen.*
A twisted offshoot to the left: *Do not place your worth
in the hands of another, you are not an offering.*
A zigzag parting: *There may be wolves who will try to eat
your flesh, you will not always recognise the claws*

in their clothing. Two braids intertwined:
And if the wolves should all descend like thunder,
cross the bridge and run, my love, run towards
the top of the mountain. You will find others waiting.

*Millions of slaves were taken from West Africa to Colombia at the hands of the Spanish at the start of the 16th century. Women would weave maps and secret messages into their hair, which was said to be one of the main ways that slaves were able to escape. 'Departes' was the name of the hairstyle women would initially braid into their hear to signal that they wanted to escape.

SENI SENEVIRATNE

FOR MY FATHER

It was a little like
black water, like lonely, like hungry

his boyhood. No wonder
he needed something stronger,

something, not bone-like
(though bones are strong), something

before calcium, something
to pull him away would do, something

other-worldly; a watchful eye
in the clouds, a hand pulling him towards

the old woman she would have been,
were it not for, were it not for –

Let's say he was a boy and
he walked without a mother.

Like medicine, the years
between. Long enough to dull

the first cut. Door on door
opened and closed but she was

always somewhere else,
as if winnowed to oblivion.

Perhaps doing cryptic
crosswords was all he could do.

And then again, the meticulous
polishing of his children's shoes

every Sunday evening was
another way of repairing the damage.

RUTH SUTOYÉ

OMI ÀDÚRÀ
(For B. Williams)

mother is fasting
again   she pours
holy water from
centre of my head
mother is praying
(*ibanuje sá lọ*) that
gust does not take
me where God
cannot find me
mother is singing
summoning heaven
(*sọkalẹ wà   o*
ọmọ aládé wúrà)
mother is kneeling
bruised (alàánú
ẹ ṣàánú fún wa)
weeping magdalene
tears. (olúwa jọ)
her yoruba is
headlocked tight
with glossolalia

but angels are
the best translators.

MAUREEN ROBERTS

THE CLAPPING GAME

Under the cocoa we play
the clapping game *'my mama told me'*
clap, clap *'if I was goody'*
clap, clap. The cocoa is full
maroon and ripe.

Under our feet is dappled
shade, surrounding us the sway of long green
grass waiting to be cutlassed short
again. In this time and space
there is no tomorrow.

The ground doves, sable grey,
bob up and down.
Careless of their beauty, fragile
butterflies whisper past our faces.

LYNNE E. BLACKWOOD

UNDER A CERULEAN SKY

Your waxy face floats. It's a waning moon
under a
cerulean

Californian sky. A headscarf the same hue,
tied
tight,
envelops your hairless skull, stripped by cancer.

Blues
blend
as if you are already in heaven. You want to be
alive,

bright
but a hidden canker riddles the brain, replaces
the grey
with voids,
eats a feast of synapses and neurones.

Your brain is dull, dying, gasping to find
broken
pathways

to memories through disconnected filaments.
The flow
has ceased,

our past desiccated. The veins under your
translucid
skin
are a map that form routes, traffic slowed.

'Do you remember,' I ask, 'blackberry-
picking
for jam?'

Your grey eyes flicker hedgerows, then vacant
gaze
drifts
yonder. I remember a dead crow on

the path,
alive
with squirming of white maggots easing
gorged
bodies

over a bone
and black feather
patchwork.

ROY MCFARLANE

DANCING WITH GHOSTS

Our mothers prayed before a God with three names
danced with a ghost from Pentecost
spoke in tongues and believed in the magic
of another world where ancestors danced with the spirit.

They were mothers that needed the hurt to be loved
away, needed to be loved in the absence of lovers.
The spirit entered you, loved you, caused you to buck
and wail, loved you like you'd never been loved before.

We learned to dance like our mothers of the church,
round, thin, dark, light, those with pride
who could barely talk to you and those who hugged you with love,
full breasts that absorbed you, warm bodies wrapped around you.

We danced like they did, we who had been
fed on verses and chapters from birth
and those who were new, wide-eyed
and eager to be loved, we danced to midnight
with ghosts we barely knew, went to school
the next day with kids who spoke of Lovers Rock,
Shubeen and midnight dances in front rooms.

Our mothers danced at morning prayers,
noon time singing and evening revivals.
Danced in high heels, barefoot
danced in short dresses.
Danced at births and funerals,
even the birth of Christ
and his death too.

SUMIA JUXUN

AFUR AS LAST SUPPER

(After Momtaza Mehri's 'Biscotti Boys/ On Men Who Wear Living
as Loosely as Their Suits')

In this dream/ every boy is in attendance/ even the ones we
already prayed over/ each carrying a plate from his mother/
wrapped in foil/ for a while no one speaks/ each reacquainting
his body
>   /to the memory of living
>   /to what his mother's hands have made.
We argue over what time fast breaks/ each swears by the app
on his phone as his Bible/ when the *Adhan* goes off/ each hand
reaches forth like an old routine. Xaawo's son leans too/ continues
a conversation that has grown seven years since we last saw him
>   /traded tight curls for a retreating hairline since then
>   /traded a room in UB3 for one at Belmarsh since then
>   /in this dream/ his voice is dancing
>   /wearing all its teeth.
A bowl full of *maraq* sits in the middle/ bone drenched in liquid/
the skin on Ilyas' back tightens/ with a memory it denies/ somewhere
in Rotterdam a phone silently vibrates/ the liquid loops in and out
of his body/ in this dream/ his hands trace the beginning of yours/
reassurance that /you
>   /we are very much alive…
For a moment/ we forget how it ends/ deep burgundy *shah*/ or Vimto
sits/ between each pair of knees
>   /& spills.

93

SAMATAR ELMI

FROM A FATHER TO A DAUGHTER

( )

Your mother wants the poems about you;
fatherhood-bildungsroman-eulogies,
clever villanelles where, like you, the refrain
reinvents the stanzas of our narrative,
a reassuring haven for us to return to.
She wants sonnets that mirror the paradox
between finite space and infinite odds,
fit for you, our living breathing dialectic.
But I haven't any poems, save fragments
that can't hold a candle to the lyric
of your light and yet I try and try
to find a box that can hold the sun.

♫

Once, I lived in semi-quavers, alternating
rhythm – spiral waltzes and dizzy 5/4,
a mid-eight that passed like an absence seizure,
the fruits of a cherry glowing in an overgrown
ashtray, self-flagellation by eight-track mixers
and shit EQs, the torture of striking a balance
with little more than an out-of-tune piano.
Miriam, you're too young to understand now,
but you're the breve in every bar, *pianississimo,*
the gift of common time for a restless mind.
You are chronograph, sundial, my crutch –
your voice carries the libretto to our opera.
I swear to God you're too young to understand,
mother of my harmony, my *anno domini.*

π

I am your father but you made me a son.
I held your hands as we learned to walk.
Your first parroted words reimagined
my lexicon, the imbued semiotics
of *dada, mama, Mimi* – no longer a string
of morphemes but the first bricks of Babel
where we built our modest temple.

Your gargled *gagaga*, which we learned
was the purest expression of love –
became our prayer at the altar.

Soon you'll decorate the walls of our temple
with icons of that scribbled stick family,
dada, mama, Mimi, immortalised,
for as long our temple survives.

ROGER ROBINSON

REPAST

With my child fighting every day to live,
the sliver and thin skin of him,
I ate. At first, in celebration he'd lived another day,
but quickly to something else – a hunger,
so insatiable, so rabid.
I took tips from the Indian nurses. Held the softest roti
folded in layers between my fingers,
salivated over pink plastic bowls of beef,
oil grease floating to the top,
chilli pepper stinging my lips and tongue.
Leaving the hospital car park with my son alive
another day – no deadly dips in oxygen,
and no sluggish heartbeats –
felt like a celebration. Who knew what we'd face
from the consultant and students on morning rounds –
a bad night, a brain hemorrhage, a death?
Eating felt like celebration, a reset, release.
Cooks began to know my first name.
I tried whole menus, saffran-coloured pillau rice
grains sticking in my beard. I'd clear my wife's plate.
I'd wake unable to sleep, boil four eggs and toast
half a loaf with butter melting on each slice; roasted
whole chickens stuffed with thyme, and ate
it all, a hunger and thirst like none other, tonguing threads
of beef wedged between my teeth. My lips glistening
with ghee.

RAYMOND ANTROBUS

MY MOTHER REMEMBERS
(*Lives / strung out like beads before me* – Grace Nichols)

serving Robert Plant, cheeky bugger,
tried to haggle my prices down.
I didn't care about velvet nothing,
I'm just out in snow on a Saturday market morning
trying to make rent and this is it;
when you're raised poor the world is touched
different, like you have to feel something, know it
with your hand, you need to know what is
worth what to who. I've served plonkers
in my time. That singer, Seal, tried to croon
my prices down, I was like, *No no,*
I'm one missed meal away from misery, mate!
I used to squat in abandoned factories,
go to jumble sales and come home to piece
together this cupboard, filling it with fabrics.
Then I met this wood sculptor, had these tree-trunk
forearms, he said, *Why not go to*
Camden Passage on Wednesday?
I had this van, made twenty-eight quid.
Look, everything I sold is listed in this notebook.
Fabrics, cleaned from your great gran's house.
Vintage. People always reach back to times
gone and that's what I'm saying,
people want to carry the past. Make it
fit them, make it say, *This is still us.*
I'd take sewn dresses made in the '20s –
your great gran was a dressmaker,
you know, dresses carried her. I wore
this white and green thing to
her funeral. Sorry, guess everything
has its time. Are you ready to eat
or am I holding you up?

AKILA RICHARDS

THE GIVERS

My mother's eastern eyes stand out
in mine. Closed, they observe the unseen.

My father's southern lips draw in unspoken
longing, translated in my first tongue-tied kiss.

My mother's mother's Nordic hands hug me till grown,
then her ashes migrate under sea, extending in orange soil.

My father's mother lends me her stretched thighs
re-birthing east, south, north and the rest.

My hands open my eyes, stroke my lips and lift my thighs.
They love each other well, even if the givers don't.

NIKHEEL GOROLAY

MLANGO (DOOR)

I have a sculpted body:
carved into shape
by generations of trade.

From my vanilla-vine veins
to my fish-scale nails,
I've thrived on the exchange
and sale of goods.

I'm the progeny of many odysseys,
the seed of ocean-crossing merchantry.
Suckled on sunburnt breasts over centuries
I'm the first and last born of this community.

And like chunks of meat
skewered as mushkaki
this port city sells my flesh
to show its love for me.

Nothing tastes like me:
a spice-infused history –
once a foreign Mhindi
now a local Swahili.

AISHA PHOENIX

SEASONS OF THE CLOTH

At a roadside stall in Dakar one spring, I picked
fabric. Asked a tailor to fashion me

　　　　　a dress the colour of the sea around my mother's island
with a constellation of stars. The following summer, I wore that
dress
As my belly swelled
And I grew slow
And heavy.
Like a ripe watermelon

　　　　　　　　　I was cut open and you were born.

Dadi Ma went to Delhi in the autumn,
Bought you red and green kurtas.
You looked majestic,
Embroidered with gold leaves.

　　　　　　　　　Now winter's here,
　　　　　　　the season of Disney princesses –

　　　　　Frozen. You wear machine-stitched costumes
　　　　　　　　　Like everyone else.
　　　　　　　　　They leave me cold,
　　　　　But I think of Dakar; hope for spring.

SELINA RODRIGUES

JEERA SINGS

The last bus to the sea left an hour ago.
Pricked stars. Is the dark darker when it's cold?

Fine English rain sparks in the streetlight;
people here are flat-boned and white

in lace-talk, waltzing in snakeskin and pearls
as drink-tight boys grin and curl

their smoke around girls. I'm mapless – my attempt
at losing signals, at displacement,

as white cousins told me. Not my face but somewhere
deeper I'm fading. Where is Little India

the tinfoil palace of every small town,
of every tumultuous city, the one

that singes the air with jeera and holds
Ganesh amongst ladoos and marigolds?

Searching branches, my feather hand's missing
the family tree, the curved foreign writing.

Between windswept stone, the sticky take-away
holds the locals in heat, but no-one escapes

from their roots. Everyone looks back and carries
        their village on their back, to the next village.

ROMMI SMITH

ROOM OF MIRRORS
(*For Ali Hussein*)

You ask when I left there. Well, I remember
not the year,
nor the month,
but the feeling

as the time when
the System put a sold-sign on my freedom
and a nightmare ran naked through the streets of my imagining,
chanting its name in capitals: Numeiri. Numeiri Numeiri:,نُميرى

When I arrived here I sat at a table with a plain white cloth.
Ate a meal in courses. Sanctuary. Picked up the strange cutlery –
but like an impulse put it down:

used the right hand, as we'd always done.
And as I scooped mouthfuls, I wept. Time. Grief.
No moloukhiah: ملّوخيه. ; no mafroukat: مفروكات no ho' b:حُب

On the late-night bus passing through hostile streets,
I looked for mirrors – but there were none. But I began
a testament to thinking.
Writing. Being Here.

Sang a thirty-year-long lullaby –
for Sudan;
a pariah on the world's slip road
mouthing its unheard psalm.

When the sky changed
and grew birds
with dream-long wings
in delicate lower-case,

I returned,
not with a boy's,
but a man's voice.

It's strange: a plane ticket buying you time,
backwards, down a tunnel of years
to arrive
outside your childhood home

— an ark to longing;
a museum to belonging.
The same metal washing line
holding up the sky!

In my suitcase photos of my English wife.

A man searching for his own reflection
unbolts the dark to find there are mirrors in a room.
Each one contains a long-lost face, but older;
brother, sisters, cousins and at their hips,
smaller, younger versions of them, unknown.

Like the skin's blueprint or echo made flesh —
that's Sa' da: صعدا in my language — their faces, a gift,

a freeze-frame of all the missing years.

SUDEEP SEN

ANTHROPOCENE

Climate change poses a powerful challenge to what is perhaps the single most important political conception of the modern era: the idea of freedom, which is central not only to contemporary politics but also to the humanities, the arts and literature.
— AMITAV GHOSH, *The Great Derangement: Climate Change and the Unthinkable*

Heat Sand

Heat outside is like latticed sand on my skin —
swift, sharp, pointed, deceptive and very hot.

The dry atmosphere simmers, sears, scorches
living tissues alive — greens to dead brown —

melting street tarmac into viscous volcanic glue.
UV rays refract swiftly through the air —

this city, a glistening glassy mirage, fuming,
fulminating, frothing — with a deathly touch.

* * *

Pollution

   Neem's serrated leaves
outside my study

   cannot hide
the mutating of seasons

on her skin –
the arterial passages

weighing time
as damaged warts

and leaf-ridges
struggle to supply air

to her pale-green lungs.
Even the air

outside is not enough
to sustain her life

anymore –
the neem that once

was a filter for us,
now needs one herself.

*

RUTH SUTOYÉ

EARS THE SHAPE OF THE WIND
(After Caleb Femi)

boy, black with cloud hair / says thunder is his papa's voice / turn
thunder's skin inside out/ my father sounds more like this.

black boy with wool mane / says his papa's voice is God-loud /
gut loud of his audacity and furore / as in scrape clean the belly of
the sky of all its rain /as in my father's voice is a drought.

boy, black with Afro puffs and owl eyes / memorised the sheet
music of his papa's tone / skipping notes never / all trumpet
laden and talking drums on fire.

there must be a carnival in the trunk of his papa's throat /
what it is to recognise a song.

~~
~~
~~

On the eves when sea smells like blood and regret
I hear her ghost singing along with King Sunny Ade.
She is always a tenor
                    (I am a tenor)
with a cyclone voice, forcing proud mountains to their knees
twisting ears of trees to submission.

                    I have never imagined her gentle.

VICTORIA ADUKWEI BULLEY

TERMINAL INDEX

So far, what I have
is you, Dad, migrating
from sitting room, bottom right-hand
side of the house, two floors skywards
to the loft, then back earthbound
to catch signal

Hello!
Oonu nhe? Oonu nhe?

can you hear me?

And though my sides split and
leak laughs onto the internet
at this telecom farce, I will know
what that phrase means
for what's left of my life.

And then you, Mum, downstairs
with a more local transmission
phone warm at your cheeks'
clan marks, now transmitters
breathing

Oo wɔhiɛ mliŋ

I am well.
God is good

or you, Mum, with me
on the floor of the kitchen
my kneecap a bar of soap ablaze
my mouth a chimney of howl
and your

　　　kpo... kpo...

conjured to end pain
unspill milk, or unspool thread
tied too tautly around a bale
of braided hair.

So far, my menagerie of terms is
small fragment, speck, found object
sound, word and phonic
but I keep it.

Collect, collect, collate
and conceal it – under head and pillow
just as Grandma caches money
in case she ever needs it.
In case it one day grows.

NANA-ESSI J. CASELY-HAYFORD

FRETWORK IN MY SPIRIT

Everyone called her Aaatii.
An intriguing maze of knowledge woven
from experience over time. Imparting
necessaries whilst encouraging me to
embrace the wild woman in me
as well as relish every representation
of remoteness afforded a medicine woman.
The hallowed she-weft and warp of
ancient and current know-how.

She who taught me my first
threading together of Job *enisua*
to adorn the *Chɛkɛrɛ* that hangs
on the side of my bookcase today.
Armed with awls of varied sizes,
twining closely slatted cane for
basketry weaving, beading
secrets and dreams into being.

She was a living ornament accessorised
with rare beads and cowrie shells that
spoke languages of divination, premonition and healing.
Materfamilias of multi-dimensions
scented with *kurobo* and lemon grass.
Born in the 1800s instructing in parquetry
into the twenty-first century.

Her algorithmic astuteness percussing
vibrations coursing through a bloodline
that stretched beyond a century's expectations.
She was elegant in her stance against
patriarchal meshes that would thwart womanhood

watching, listening, paying attention to the
messages around her – passing them on to me.
I welcome the *apakan* of grace she set out for me to ride
from whose height I can view and query
mysteries of the past including horizons of the future.
My mother's mother, my Aaatii
a fretwork in my spirit.

TISHANI DOSHI

MY GRANDMOTHER NEVER ATE A POTATO IN HER LIFE

I can't be sure, but I like the shock
of it, the irrationality
of not wanting to harm the unseen
bacteria underground.
The abstinence of tuber.
My grandmother (even though
I was told never to begin
a poem with grandmother)
wore big glasses and enjoyed
diamonds and cards. She made
deer of her fingers, and peacocks.
As a girl she wore ribbons
in her plaits. I miss her even though
it has been so long since I knew her.
I think of her great care towards ants,
of the shiny coins she slipped me.
Of the words I take from her mouth
and paste into imaginary notebooks.
The TV blares and my brother reclines
like a baby god, watching cartoons,
straining his fragile neck.
We are in the house alone together
and it is everything I've ever feared.
The soft night of Madras pushing
her sweaty chest towards us,
saying, see how alone,
you and him and her.

BARSA RAY

BLOOD LOSS

My menstrual blood flows free until I read the eulogy.
Grief turns, a red soufflé rising within;
each morning, the thud of a meteorite,
its force-chain absorbed; on opening my eyes,
I swallow the burning urge to run.
Why chafe on losing blood I don't have,
with so much to pluck from the air?
Every plate, cup, glass, vase,
picture, screen, chair smashed.
Floating fissile yield;
pillows, quilts, spewing fly-ash,
in the shaken snow globe of our home.
I labour to sort, join, glue, wait and wait
for the bonds to dry, to recreate the corpus of our life
from the fragments, the corpuscles,
watching veins form from the joins, clumped sutures,
so long in fusing, and still no surface smooth,
unaware of coming to term, until the blood surges,
and nine months from drying up,
I birth my grief.

RAYMOND ANTROBUS

ODE TO MY HAIR

When a black woman
with straightened hair
looks at you, says,

Nothing black about you,
do you rise like wild wheat?
A dark field of frightened strings?

For years I hide you under hats
and still, cleanly, you cling to my scalp
conceding nothing

when they call you too soft,
too thin for the texture
of your own roots.

Look, the day is shea butter yellow,
the night is my Jamaican cousin
saying *Your skin and hair mean*

you're treated better than us,
the clippings of a hot razor
trailing the back of my neck.

O scissor the voice of the barber
who charges more to cut
this thick tangle of Coolie.

Now you've grown a wildness,
are you trying to be my father's 'fro
to grow him out, so I can see him again?

KEITH JARRETT

PARASITES

When I was twenty-one or maybe it was
twenty-two amoebas multiplied the pain of it

I left for home lighter much lighter though tropical
sun turned my shade to black my own mother didn't

last year at the hospital lab parasites rediscovered
in my stools sit with this a little while so much time

hidden settling unsettling one is transitive one in-transit
I am saying only what those microscopes saw not what I

felt so much so many years of unsettling so gut me in my
feeling so many poisoned rivers so sad when they said unto

me I had been carrying these Caribbean waters all these years
gut refugees fed an old world diet I will not say contaminated

I would rather carry a billion billion times more because I am hosting
their stories and I have never felt this empty this bitter this so help me.

SUI ANUKKA

IN MY MOTHER

Neurotransmitters blow

explode out of existence
land dead, on a map,
in a constellation
floating in amniotic fluid –

an intricate weave of
possibilities
I hide in plain sight
avoiding the careless
violence of my maker.

Found out, I cannot
escape her imprint.
Fear-marked, shame-scarred,
branded, I learn to
preach silences.
I turn on her then. I let go.
And when we part
I leave no traces
of my complex congregation
on her body nation.

BIOGRAPHIES

Tolu Agbelusi is a Nigerian British writer, performer, educator and lawyer. A Callaloo Fellow, she's been published internationally, commissioned widely, led guest lectures to PhD students at Birbeck University and is working towards her first poetry pamphlet.

Raymond Antrobus is a British-Jamaican poet from Hackney, East London. He is the author of *To Sweeten Bitter* and *The Perseverance*. He is the recipient of fellowships from Cave Canem and Complete Works 3. He has an MA in Spoken Word Education from Goldsmiths. In 2018 he was awarded The Geoffrey Dearmer Prize.

Sui Anukka is a Manchester based writer. Her work has been published in the Commonword anthologies: *Elevator Fiction* and *Sounds that Exceed 80 Decibels*. Sui is part of the Commonword Women in the Spotlight Programme. She is a graduate of the University of Bristol and the National Film and Television School.

Lynne E. Blackwood is a disabled Anglo-Indian writer of poetry, plays, stories, novels – who loves performance. Her stories feature in *Closure*, *Asian Writer*, *Brighton Prize* anthologies, amongst others. She's being mentored by The Literary Consultancy for her collection based on her Anglo-Indian family history. Her second novel was a WriteNow 2017 finalist.

Siddhartha Bose's books include two poetry collections, *Kalagora* and *Digital Monsoon*, a monograph on the grotesque, *Back and Forth*, and a play, *No Dogs, No Indians*. His theatre work includes *Kalagora*, *London's Perverted Children*, and *The Shroud*. In 2011-2013 he was a Leverhulme Fellow in Drama at the University of London.

Victoria Adukwei Bulley is a British-born Ghanaian poet and writer. A former Barbican Young Poet, her work has been commissioned by the Royal Academy of Arts in addition to being featured on BBC Radio 4. Her first pamphlet, *Girl B*, edited by Kwame Dawes, was published in 2017.

Michael Campbell is a poet, illustrator and aspiring author. His first poetry collection, *I am not myself*, was published by Sunesis Ministries Ltd. Michael is also working on a novel. He has a BA in Animation and a Masters in English Literature.

Nana-Essi Josephine Casely-Hayford is a storyteller and writer who works as a part-time Writing for Wellbeing Practitioner with Keighley Library – (Bradford Libraries) where she facilitates Positive Wellbeing and Expressive Visualisation through the Arts.

Maya Chowdhry's writing is infused and influenced through her poetic work for radio, film, theatre and digital. Her poetry collections are *Fossil* (2016, Peepal Tree Press) and *The Seamstress and the Global Garment* (2009, Crocus). Her digital poetic work 'Ripple' was shortlisted for the 2015 Dot Award.

Rishi Dastidar is a fellow of The Complete Works, a consulting editor at *The Rialto*, a member of Malika's Poetry Kitchen, and chair of writer development organisation, Spread The Word. His debut collection is *Ticker-tape* (Nine Arches Press), from which a poem was included in *The Forward Book of Poetry 2018*.

Tishani Doshi is an award-winning poet, novelist and dancer. Her most recent book, *Girls Are Coming Out of the Woods* (Bloodaxe Books), is a PBS summer recommendation, a powerful collection of poems, which deal with coastal living, gender violence, memory, happiness, ageing, and what the point of poetry might be. She lives on a beach in Tamil Nadu with her husband and three dogs.

Zena Edwards is a writer, Live Literature Artist, Arts Activist and Project developer. She is co-founder of 'Voices That Shake!' – a youth arts, race and power project and is the creative and educational Director of 'Verse In Dialogue'. Her work centres on issues of rehumanising marginalised voices, climate, the environment and social justice.

Samatar Elmi has been shortlisted for the Venture Award, New Generation African Poets, the Complete Works II and is a graduate of the Young Inscribe Mentoring Program. Poems have appeared in *Magma*, *Iota*, *Scarf*, *Ink Sweat and Tears*, *Myths of the Near Future*, the *Echoing Gallery* and *Cadaverine*.

Christina Fonthes is a Congolese-British writer. Her poetry, laden with themes of womanhood and sexuality has featured in several publications including *Ake Review*. Her mantra 'telling stories through any means possible' allows her to bring untold stories to life through writing, performance and digital art.

Patricia Foster McKenley is an award-winning poet, international performer, Inscribe contracted writer, co-host for 'At The Inkwell London' reading series, and 'Malika's Poetry Kitchen' alumni. She's released a poetry film, 'LIPS' and honoured at 'TO-GETHER WE RISE' Women's Awards for Poetry Services (2015). As SABLE Poet in residence she participated in the Mboka Festival in The Gambia, 2017.

Kat François is a performance artist, educator, playwright, director and personal trainer. She is a BBC and World poetry slam champion. Her play 'Raising Lazarus', on Caribbean soldiers in WW1, tours internationally. Kat teaches dance, poetry, drama and performance skills and contributes to BBC Radio 4's *Front Row* and *Woman's Hour*.

Nandita Ghose's poetry has been published in *Southbank*, *Magma*, *X-Press* and the *Wolf* magazines, and in the anthology *The Iron Book of Humorous Verse*. Her poem 'This Nose' won first prize for the funniest poem in the Edinburgh Fringe 2003. She has written plays for BBC Radio 4 and for TV.

Nikheel Gorolay has had poetry and book reviews published in *SABLE* LitMag and is currently redrafting his first novel. He holds an MA from School of Oriental and African Studies (SOAS), University of London, where he researched representations of British womanhood in late nineteenth century India.

Maggie Harris is a Guyana-born writer. She has twice won the Guyana Prize for Literature and was Regional Winner of the Commonwealth Short Story Prize for 'Sending for Chantal'. Her latest fiction is *Writing on Water*, (Seren) and *Sixty Years of Loving*, (Cane Arrow Press).

Joshua Idehen is a poet, teacher and musician. A British born Nigerian, he recently collaborated with The Comet Is Coming on their Mercury-nominated debut album *Channel the Spirits* and MOBO award-winning Sons of Kemet. He is touring a second album with the band Benin City, *Last Night*.

Keith Jarrett, former UK poetry slam champion and Rio International Poetry Slam winner 2014, is a PhD scholar at Birkbeck University, where he is completing his first novel. His monologue, 'Safest Spot in Town', has been aired on BBC Four. His book of poetry, *Selah*, was published in 2017.

Sumia Juxun is a Barbican Young Poet Alumni and Fourhubs' 2018 Poetry Prize Winner. A linguist and programmer, she often facilitates coding and writing workshops in secondary schools, festivals and Keats House's Creative Writing Summer School.

Pete Kalu's art runs to film-making, coding and flash fiction. He can tightrope walk and led a carnival band called Moko Jumbies – Ghosts of the Gods.

Fawzia Muradali Kane was born in Trinidad & Tobago, and practices as an architect in London. Her first collection of poetry *Tantie Diablesse* (Waterloo Press 2011) was a poetry finalist for the 2012 Bocas Lit Fest prize. A pamphlet *Houses of the Dead* was published by Thamesis in 2014.

Rachel Long is a poet and facilitator. Her poems have featured in *Magma*, *The London Magazine*, and *The Honest Ulsterman*. She is assistant tutor on the Barbican Young Poets programme, and leader of Octavia – a poetry collective for women of colour, housed at Southbank Centre, London.

Adam Lowe is a writer, publisher and performer from Leeds (though he now lives in Manchester). He is LGBT History Month Poet Laureate.

Nick Makoha is a Cave Canem Graduate Fellow & Complete Works Alumni. He won the 2015 Brunel International Poetry prize and the 2016 Toi Derricotte & Cornelius Eady Chapbook Prize for his pamphlet *Resurrection Man*. His *Kingdom of Gravity* (Peepal Tree, 2017) was shortlisted for the Forward Prize.

Roy McFarlane was born in Birmingham of Jamaican parentage and has been Birmingham's Poet Laureate. Roy's contributed to *Out of Bounds* (Bloodaxe 2012) and he's the writer and editor of *Celebrate Wha?* (Smokestack 2011). His first poetry collection, *Beginning With Your Last Breath*, was published by Nine Arches Press (2018).

Momtaza Mehri is a poet, essayist and editor. She is a Complete Works Fellow and co-winner of the 2018 Brunel International African Poetry Prize and the 2017 Out-spoken Page Poetry Prize. She is the Young People's Laureate for London (2018) and columnist-in-residence at the San Francisco Museum of Modern Art's Open Space.

Sai Murray's first poetry collection *Ad-liberation*, was published in 2013. He was lead writer on Virtual Migrants 2015 touring production, Continent Chop Chop and runs artist/activist promotions agency Liquorice Fish. He is a poet facilitator on

Voices that Shake!; a Numbi resident poet; and arts and politics editor of *SABLE Lit Mag*.

Selina Nwulu is a writer, poet and essayist. Her first chapbook *The Secrets I Let Slip* was published by Burning Eye Books and is a Poetry Book Society recommendation. She writes for several outlets such as the *Guardian*, *New Humanist* and *Red Pepper*. She was Young Poet Laureate for London 2015-16.

Louisa Adjoa Parker writes poetry, fiction and on black history. Her first poetry collection *Salt-sweat and Tears* was published by Cinnamon Press, who also published her pamphlet *Blinking in the Light*. Louisa's work has appeared in various publications, including *Wasafiri*, *Envoi*, *Out of Bounds*, *Under the Radar* and *Bare Fiction*.

Aisha Phoenix writes poetry and stories. Her work appears in the *Bath Flash Fiction Anthology*, *Litro USA* online and *Word Riot*. She studies MA Creative Writing at Birkbeck and has a PhD in Sociology. As an undergraduate at Oxford she was part of the Slice ( ) Mango poetry collective.

Barsa Ray's poems have been filmed for the Yorkshire Arts Festival, performed at the Ilkley Literature Festival, published in *Inkposts*, *The Telegraph Sunday Magazine* (Calcutta) and *The Brainwave*. She was shortlisted in *The Asian Writer* First Novel competition. She is an Inscribe writer currently writing her second novel.

Akila Richards is a published writer, poet and spoken word artist. She performs and reads in a range of settings including internationally. Recent work appeared in digital animation and printed on clothes in a collective exhibition. She has written a play based on her short story, 'Secret Chamber', published in *Closure*.

Maureen Roberts is Senior Development Officer at London Metropolitan Archives and curates the 'Word on the Street' arts festival. She managed Keats House Museum and is a Trustee of

Black Cultural Archives. Her first poetry collection, *My Grandmother Sings to Me* was published by Bogle-L'Ouverture Publications.

Roger Robinson is a writer who has performed worldwide and is an experienced workshop leader and lecturer in poetry. He was chosen by Decibel as one of 50 writers who have influenced the Black British writing canon.

Selina Rodrigues' poetry has been published in a number of journals and her book will be published by Smokestack Books. She is an experienced performer and has been Poet in Residence at Open Square Gardens and the Poetry School. Selina is of Indian/ English parentage and she writes about identity and the push-pull of behaviour and desire.

Sudeep Sen's prize-winning books include *Postmarked India: New & Selected Poems*, *Rain*, *Aria*, *The HarperCollins Book of English Poetry* (editor), *Fractals: New & Selected Poems / Translations 1980-2015*, and *EroText*. Sen is the first Asian honoured to speak and read at the Nobel Laureate Festival. The Government of India awarded him the senior fellowship for "outstanding persons in the field of culture/literature".

Seni Seneviratne is a writer and multi-disciplinary creative artist. She has collaborated with film makers, visual artists, musicians and digital artists. Her most recent collaboration, 'Lady of Situations', combined poetry, theatre, digital art and music. Her latest poetry collection is, *The Heart of It* (Peepal Tree Press). www.seniseneviratne.com

Ioney Smallhorne is studying an MA in Creative Writing/ Education at Goldsmiths University. She is also a filmmaker and enjoys translating her poems to the screen. When not writing, she is failing her motorbike test, growing vegetables, travelling, learning Italian and working at Nottingham Black Archive.

Rommi Smith is a poet, playwright and performer with numerous prestigious residencies for organisations from the British Council to the BBC. Inaugural Poet-in-Residence for British Parliament and the Inaugural-Writer-in-Residence for Keats House, Smith is John Barnard Scholar at Leeds University and a visiting scholar at City University New York.

Degna Stone, an Inscribe supported writer, is a co-founder of *Butcher's Dog* poetry magazine and a contributing editor at *The Rialto*. She received a Northern Writers Award in 2015 and is a fellow of The Complete Works III. Appearances include StAnza International Poetry Festival and BBC Radio 3s The Verb.

Hugh Stultz is a Fundraising Consultant with Safe Ground, an arts organisation. Hugh's poetry has been published in the UK and Jamaica. Hugh studied at the Jamaica School of Drama and Goldsmiths College and cites his drama background for the recurring performance motif within his poetry.

Ruth Sutoyé is a poet, creative producer and visual artist. She is a Roundhouse Resident Artist, Barbican Young Poet alumni and member of the SXWKS collective. Her work has featured in several publications and platforms including *Opus*, *True Africa*, *Bad Betty Press* and The Cob Gallery.

Keisha Thompson is a Manchester based writer, performance artist and producer. She works at Contact managing the Contact Young Company. Most recently, she received a co-commission from STUN and Contact to develop her new solo show, 'Man on the Moon'. Her debut book, *Lunar* (40 poems and 'The Man on the Moon' script), was published in 2018.

Gemma Weekes is an interdisciplinary writer/poet, musicmaker and performer. Author of critically-acclaimed novel, *Love Me* (Chatto & Windus), and chapbook *I Can Only Fix You if You Break*, she is currently working on a new immersive stage piece, her second novel, and several scripts for TV & film.

Indigo Williams is a British Nigerian poet from South London. She is the founder of 'I Shape Beauty' blog and has performed at events and venues such as: BBC Radio 4's 'Bespoken Word', The Royal Shakespeare Company and Glastonbury.

Dorothy Wang is Professor in the American Studies Program and Faculty Affiliate in the English Department at Williams College (Massachusetts). Her monograph, *Thinking Its Presence: Form, Race, and Subjectivity in Contemporary Asian American Poetry* (Stanford University Press, 2013), received the Association for Asian American Studies' award for best book of literary criticism in 2016, garnered honorable mention in the Poetry Foundation's inaugural Pegasus Awards for Criticism in 2014, and was named one of *The New Yorker*'s 'The Books We Loved in 2016'. The first national conference on race and creative writing in the United States was named 'Thinking Its Presence' and was convened in 2014, 2015, and 2017 at the University of Montana (twice) and the University of Arizona. Wang conceived of and co-founded the 'Race and Poetry and Poetics in the UK' (RAPAPUK) research initiative, which held its second conference at Queens' College, Cambridge University, in October 2018. She has also published on Asian Australian literature.

Nii Ayikwei Parkes is a novelist, poet, broadcaster and editor. He is the author of the book of poems *The Makings of You* and the hybrid novel, *Tail of the Blue Bir*d, which is translated into Dutch, German, Spanish, French, Italian, Catalan and Japanese. The French translation of the novel won the 2014 Prix Baudelaire, Prix Mahogany and Prix Laure Bataillon and was selected by leading literary magazine LIRE as the Best First Foreign Book of the year in 2014. He is a 2007 recipient of Ghana's ACRAG award for poetry and literary advocacy. He writes for children under the name K. P. Kojo and is the founder and senior editor at flipped eye publishing. In 2014, he was selected as one of Africa's 39 most promising authors of the new generation for the World Book Capital Africa 39 Project and he is the current producer of Literature and Talks at the Brighton Dome & Festival.

Kadija (George) Sesay, FRSA, is the Publications Manager for the Inscribe Programme for Peepal Tree Press. She is the founder/publisher of SABLE LitMag, SABLE LitFest, and co-founder of The Mboka Festival of Arts, Culture and Sport in The Gambia. She is the editor of several anthologies of work by writers of African and Asian descent and her poetry collection, *Irki* (Peepal Tree Press, 2013) was shortlisted for the Glenna Luschei Prize for African Poetry in 2014. She received an Arts Council England grant for Research and Development for her second collection, The Modern Pan Africanist's Journey and produced an app based on it, *The Modern Pan Africanist's Journey*. http://www.sablelitmag.org/mpajweb1/webapp/

Kadija has received several awards for her work in the Creative Arts. She is a Fellow of the George Bell Institute, a Fellow of the Kennedy Arts Centre of Performance Arts Management. She is a postgraduate AHRC /TECHNE scholarship researcher on Black British Publishers at Brighton University. She's also received a re-search scholarship for the Library of Congress (Washington DC) for 2019.

Red: Contemporary Black British Poetry
Isbn 9781845231293; pp. 252; pub. 2010; £9.99
Edited by Kwame Dawes

'Perhaps the most significant thing to be said about *Red* is that the poets in this volume burst through any constraining label with writing that throbs and pulses and seeps and flows.' Margaret Busby

Featuring:
Jackie Kay, Patience Agbabi, Nii Ayikwei Parkes, Raman Mundair, Maya Chowdhry, Dorothea Smartt, Fred D'Aguiar, Linton Kwesi Johnson, Bernardine Evaristo, Roi Kwabena, John Lyons, Lemn Sissay, Grace Nichols, Jack Mapanje, Daljit Nagra, John Agard, Gemma Weekes, Wangui Wa Goro and many more...

Red collects poems that engage 'red', poems by Black British poets writing with the word "red" in mind – as a kind of leap-off point, a context, a germ – the way something small, minor, or grand might spur a poem. It offers the reader the freedom to come to whatever conclusions they want to about what writing as a poet who is also Black and British might mean.

The result is a book of poets ranging from well established and published writers to first time poets. *Red* does find its usual associations with blood, violence, passion, and anger. Sometimes it is linked with sensuality and sexuality. But there are surprises, when red defines a memory or mood, the quality of light in a sky, the colour of skin, the sound of a song, and much, much more. The anthology, therefore, succeeds in producing poems that seem to be first about image, and only then about whatever else fascinates the poet.

In this sense, *Red* is a different kind of anthology of Black British writing, and the richness of the entries, the moods, the humour, the passion, the reflection, the confessional all confirm that Black British poetry is a lively and defining force in Britain today.

Editor Kwame Dawes is a poet, novelist, playwright and critic. His work as an organiser and deliverer of poetry workshops has been hailed in many parts of the world, not least in the UK, USA and Jamaica, where he is the Literary programmer of the Calabash International Literature Festival.

Closure: Contemporary Black British Short Stories
Isbn: 9781845232887; pp. 272; pub. 2015; £9.99
Edited by Jacob Ross

Closure has a variety of forms, styles and a rich diversity of theme. As a title "Closure" invited a subversive response from contributors, and this anthology is filled with stories which, like life, rarely end in the way we might expect...

"Opening a short story anthology, there is often something to delight, something to surprise. There is also often something clever, self-indulgent, that speaks of a writer's skill but limited experience of life. Jacob Ross's careful selection of stories from black British writers restores a sense of connection with the detail of human fragility in our fragmented contemporary culture; with narrative, with the spirit. With the subtle, sometimes unconscious, responses of these writers to what Britishness means. This book is both an important contribution to the future development of the form and a celebration of some of our finest writing. Surprising, delightful and full of life."

— Cathy Galvin, Director www.thewordfactory.tv, and the associate editor at *Newsweek*.

Featuring short stories by:
Monica Ali, Dinesh Angelo Allirajah, Muli Amaye, Lynne E. Blackwood, Judith Bryan, Nana-Essi Casely-Hayford, Jacqueline Clarke, Jacqueline Crooks, Fred D'Aguiar, Sylvia Dickinson, Bernardine Evaristo, Gaylene Gould, Michelle Inniss, Valda Jackson, Pete Kalu, Patrice Lawrence, Jennifer Nansubuga Makumbi, Tariq Mehmood, Raman Mundair, Sai Murray, Chantal Oakes, Karen Onojaife, Koye Oyedeji, Louisa Adjoa Parker, Desiree Reynolds, Hana Riaz, Akila Richards, Leone Ross, Seni Seneviratne, Ayesha Siddiqi, Mahsuda Snaith.

Editor Jacob Ross was born in Grenada and now lives in Britain. A fellow of the Royal Society of Literature, he is the author of two novels, *Pynter Bender* and *The Bone Readers* (winner of the Jhalak Prize) and *Tell No-One About This: Collected Short Stories, 1995-2017*. He is much in demand as a leader of workshops and masterclasses on the short story.